Interpreting
the Sacred

Interpreting
the Sacred
Ways of Viewing Religion

William E. Paden

Beacon Press
Boston

Beacon Press
25 Beacon Street
Boston, Massachusetts 02108-2892

Beacon Press books
are published under the auspices of
the Unitarian Universalist Association of Congregations.

99 98 97 96   8 7 6 5 4 3

Text design by Hunter Graphics

Library of Congress Cataloging-in-Publication Data

Paden, William E.
Interpreting the sacred : ways of viewing religion / William E.
Paden.
p.   cm.
Includes bibliographical references and index.
ISBN 0-8070-7706-2 (cloth)
ISBN 0-8070-7707-0 (paper)
1. Religion. I. Title.
BL48.P215   1992
291'.01—dc20   91-12152

For Natasha

Contents

Preface   *ix*

1   Interpretive Frames   *1*

2   The Challenge: Critical Interpretations of Religion   *15*

3   As Society, So Religion   *28*

4   As the Psyche, So the Gods   *48*

5   Comparative Perspective in the Study of Religion   *67*

6   Religious Interpretations of Religion:
   Views from the Inside   *87*

7   The Contextuality of Interpretation   *110*

8   Plurality: Issues and Implications   *125*

Notes   *137*

Index   *153*

Preface

There are thousands of books that interpret religion, and each has its point of view. As in the story of the blind men describing an elephant—one arguing that it is like a rope (he holds the tail), another that it is like a wall (he is touching the side) and another that it is like a tree (he has the leg)—explanations of religion treat a vast subject from decidedly partial points of view and limited locations.

Yet we cannot get to religion—or for that matter, the world—*except* through a point of view, and what we see will inevitably be a consequence of our particular standpoint. The differences we have about religion are the results of these root differences of context and perspective.

This book, then, is not one more view or theory of religion, but proposes that it is necessary and useful to step back and become aware of the role that views and lenses themselves play in revealing a subject like this. We need to understand the different perspectives that are already in use. In doing this we must include the outlooks of both critics and insiders, as well as some of the main sociological, psychological, and comparative approaches.

Privileged, singular models of the universe—whether strictly religious or strictly scientific—can no longer be easily assumed. There are many versions of the world, depending on our glasses (which, for example, can be anything from poetic to mathematical), depending on who is viewing it, depending on which form of knowledge is being used, and depending on which cultural lens is in play. I am sure that other people besides myself have found themselves moving through varying world-interpretations in the process of growing up in an expanding pluralistic culture. What at one time was presented to us as "the world," later began to look like the point of view of a certain class of people in a certain society, or one certain approach among other approaches, or perhaps even a pernicious ideology. We realized that the world did not have to be seen *that* way. Worldviews became just that—views. Horizons continue to shift, to coexist, to be questionable.

Such transformations have also altered our thinking about religion. The biblical religions of our upbringing appear in completely different lights when looked at by means of the modern disciplines of psychology or sociology, or in the context of the teachings of Asian traditions.

Yet such a pliant universe offers the occasion not for cynicism but for plural vision. It gives us an opportunity for reflection upon the varying models which we use to organize the world of meaning. It provides a chance for self-awareness about the positioned, selective character of the language we use to describe human existence, realizing that existence gives itself back to us through the language by which we approach it.

I have been especially motivated to write this book in order to help bridge a portion of the huge, growing gap between the general reading public and professional, academic circles of "interpretation." Too often academics write only for each other. *Interpreting the Sacred*—formed out of many years of teaching undergraduate courses on the subject at the University of Vermont—attempts to present in accessible, succinct form what is usually dealt with in specialized vocabularies and spread throughout a vast and often technical literature. It also tries to bring together in one place ideas and approaches that in their own habitats are quite unconnected with each other. In order to take seriously the plurality of interpretation, the book juxtaposes points of view that are usually thought of as mutually impertinent or even contradictory. It tries to bring out and distill the essential applications of each of these in a way that will be readable for the nonspecialist.

Although this study introduces readers to some of the main forms of interpreting religion, it is not intended as a thorough survey of all theories—some will surely find their favorite ones missing. More importantly, it focuses on how the different purposes and contexts of explanations determine the nature of what is seen. An elephant will be seen differently by a zoologist, a conservationist, a circus manager, and another elephant. We may be interested in only its social patterns, its geographic diffusion, its commercial value, or the physiology of its liver. An elephant is an object for poachers and it is an object of wonder and beauty. Ultimately, it is part of the mystery of existence itself. Religion, likewise, is seen through different glasses according to varying purposes, and can be shown to be an object of many parts, textures, and functions.

My own perspective on the "elephant" (that is, religion), at least in this book, therefore offers not another particular position as such, but attempts to illustrate in an evenhanded way the nature of positions. My purpose is to create a viewpoint where multiple viewpoints can become clear, and to show how diverse "languages" describe in quite different ways a most unusual and important subject matter.

1

Interpretive Frames

Interpretation, even more than information, tells us what a thing is. This is certainly the case with religion. No facts, no data, will settle the matter of what it signifies. Religion is a result of perspective, and can be viewed from endless and opposite angles. Is it the great truth or is it the great illusion? It can be regarded with appreciation from within or with hostility from without. Through whose eyes, through what glasses, shall we see it? From what location? And if religious insiders have conflicting views, so do outsiders. Each approach seems to take its horizon as self-sufficient, and appears to inhabit a universe of its own.

Because the many views of what religion is about lie scattered and unconnected, it is hard to find a standpoint from which to describe, much less evaluate them.[1] Each is like a different language, and on the surface all the views together become a chaotic sea of disparate voices. As viewpoints proliferate the question of religion becomes a free-for-all. Multiple explanations end up side by side in a theater of mutual contradiction, neglect, and disdain.

Such disjointedness begs to be addressed and clarified. It calls out for enlarged perspective, for stepping back from side taking, for looking at the process of just how we look at religion. This book attempts to provide a place to do that.

Points of View

The first question about religion must be about the location from which we talk about it. For the point of observation will deter-

1

mine the view, the issues, and the data. We are used to thinking of religion from the standpoint of a particular culture or tradition, such as Christianity or science; yet a general study of interpretations of religion cannot presuppose the in-house issues of any single religious or anti-religious position. We therefore cannot start with the object *religion,* a word which must always carry implied quotation marks, but with the question of the contexts in which it is observed and explained. Whose religion, and whose idea of religion, are we interpreting?

Points of view about religion, whether they are religious or nonreligious, are not just forms of pure, disembodied thought, but also forms of assertion, commitment, and territory. Each approach has its investments, its societal contexts and purposes, and its audiences. Each, in this sense, speaks from a certain place, and from that location sees the whole of religion within the categories of its limited horizon. Each sees only the features of the subject which conform to its own perspective, while all the other aspects remain blurry or in the dark, of no interest, and for all purposes nonexistent.

Observation points often are fixed, singular, and defensive. Religious and academic theories alike often have such monolocational perspectives, as though it were the mark of a correct interpretation that only one position could be valid, or that there was only one foundational meaning to religion. Because of this urge to conceptually possess religion, the realm of interpretation has formed patchworks of semantic turfs whose languages are viable only to those who share them, and whose own absolute, totalizing explanations preempt the others. The absence of interaction between these approaches suggests a socio-linguistic caste system. It suggests that interpretation is linked with positionings and territories.

Traditional cultures and religions naturally assumed their own points of view to be absolute. They did not understand their standpoints to be *versions* of the world alongside others. One's own religious beliefs seemed so widely accepted and self-evidently true that they were taken not as one of several descriptions of reality, but simply as the description of reality itself. Every culture socialized its members into these scripts, into religious programs which presented fixed, incontrovertible images of the world and its foundations. Every culture saw itself as the center of the universe, creating geographies and calendars which ordered all space and time around its own sacred absolutes, its own all-satisfying spiritual orders. What could not be seen—so cohesive and authoritative were these traditional worldviews, and so innocent of genuine cross-cultural perspective—was that this "language/reality" frame was one interpretation of the world among hundreds of different ones.

To be sure, science challenged the religious models and made them appear mostly false, but in many ways it, too, perpetuated the one-model model. The nineteenth-century belief that science had now replaced religion as the source of true knowledge about the world amounted to the substitution of one lens for another, not freedom from the captivity of singular worldviews. One system of reality, empiricist and physicalist, took the place of another, biblicist and supernaturalist, and Western thought was to become locked into a horizon of issues constituted by this opposition. Either this is God's world or it is only human; either scripture is divinely inspired or it is only a historical literature. Such binary thinking still determines the options for many Westerners when they think about religion.

Stepping Back and Studying the Frames Themselves. The capacity to see one's view of the world *as* a view is a mark of contemporary thinking.[2] Such awareness creates a basis for understanding the plurality of standpoints. The moment in which the views of others come into focus arises partly through the contemplative act of stepping back from one's own perspective and recognizing that it, too, is situated. Not just perceiving the world, but perceiving *how* we perceive the world, is in some ways becoming second nature to a pluralistic, self-conscious culture.

A new world of social and cultural diversity has formed the historical setting for this self-reflective moment. The move toward pluralistic thinking is partly an effect of contact with and respect for people who have different worldviews within the same society—the city being now the image of this diversity as the town once was an image of homogeneity. The increasing awareness of global cultures has also helped create consciousness of the positioned nature of our own views, though this realization comes more slowly. Educationally, the multitude of scientific, social scientific, and humanistic ways of construing the world gives students diverse models by which to describe their existence. It is becoming more difficult to imagine any single image of the world as having a privileged, absolute status.

If with the capacity to change so many frames so rapidly the fixed universe becomes more pliable, nevertheless what seems to be a loss of absoluteness becomes at the same time an opportunity for a new kind of pluralism. For it is not that the many lenses are all wrong (though by certain empirical criteria some may be) but rather that they can be perceived now *as* alternative lenses. In this way the interpretive frames themselves—the glasses through which and by which we focus upon certain facets of the world and not others—become a necessary, important subject matter in their own right. The difference between fields of study, for example, is the difference between their lenses of perception.

The Scale Creates the Phenomenon. Acknowledging the spectrum of interpretive lenses is a starting point for understanding another important principle: that there is an intimate relationship between the *way* we look at the world and *what* it is we see going on there. As an axiom has it, "the scale creates the phenomenon."[3] To look through a microscope is to create a certain order of data and exclude other kinds, and the same is true for looking at the world through the characters of Shakespeare's plays. Our "instrument" determines what will count as "objects," as world. Our frames are built to detect galaxies or microorganisms, but ordinarily not both; colors or sounds, but ordinarily not both; psychological or geographical data, but ordinarily not both. By changing lenses we change objects. Physicists know that light will be interpretable either as waves *or* as particles depending on the type of instrument used for observing.

When it comes to construing religion the ramifications of this fact are vast.

Theories are like complex conceptual lenses or scales. They show us how to see the world from a certain angle. They show us where to look for facts. Even broader frames are what have been called paradigms, the underlying models or premises by which we interpret the world and work out our theories.[4] Paradigms are the systems of what constitute "knowledge" for a given culture. These can change, as in the shift from Newtonian to quantum physics, or from biblical to secular worldviews. Not only scientific world-views, but also religious ones, are paradigms that give coherence and meaning to certain categories ("God," "protons") that would be valueless or nonexistent in other models. A deep implication of this concept is that science itself is not a set of privileged facts about reality, thus providing a special foundation to all *other* forms of knowledge, but one of many languages through which humans organize facts and perceive the world. The physicist's quarks and Homer's gods, as one observer notes, are equally grounded in the human ability to categorize reality.[5]

Religion

The very word *religion* is itself an interpretive, prescriptive lens. Different definitions create different sets of data, different points of focus. *Religion* is not an independent subject matter just sitting there for all to see, but a *term* that its user chooses to associate with certain kinds of phenomena. If you think religion is a social affair, then that is the aspect of it that your eye will be drawn to; and if you think religion is the spirit of charity or the worship of God, then these perceptions create for you other ranges of data.

The term *religion* has been used quite differently throughout Western history.[6] The word is from the Latin *religio*, which in Roman times meant something like "sacred observance" or "piety". The ancients themselves debated what true *religio* should be. Christianity appropriated the term and saw its own worship as the true form of *religio*, but internal Christian arguments over the concept came to a head during the Reformation. Was *religio*, for example, to be equated with engaging in the sacraments of the Catholic Church or associated with the inner faith of the Protestants?

In the seventeenth century books on "the religions of the world" began to appear. *Religion* came to designate all systems of supernatural belief that were, by then, recognized to exist around the globe. Later, nineteenth-century philosophies started to interpret religion as a special, unique area of culture and experience, alongside art, politics, and other human symbol systems. A modern search for the essence of religion began in earnest, though the word had now lost its original Roman meaning of "true piety" and had become an open-ended term like *art*, practically a blank check to be filled in by any interpreter.

The term has become completely equivocal—one word, same sound and spelling, with numerous and different meanings, endlessly flexible. That there has been no agreement on definitions should give pause. That other cultures do not even have a term corresponding exactly to the Western generic *religion* should also give pause. What data shall be included or excluded as "religious?" And who is to say?

Popular uses of the word *religion* tend to be loaded with either positive or negative judgment. For the average person it still means their own religion—or the one they have rejected. Religion is thus "going to church," "believing in the Qur'an," "praying the rosary," "loving your neighbor," or even "a way of life;" but it is also "social show," "money-grabbing," "fanaticism," or "brainwashing." It is "the worship of the true God," but also "an emotional crutch." Even the expression *interpreting religion* may be quickly and automatically associated with internal matters like the Church's views on abortion or the problems of keeping a kosher home. In ordinary linguistic contexts the term carries decidedly local applications and associations.

In contrast, the comparative study of religion,[7] now a standard part of university pursuits, has uncovered striking, definition-defying diversities, corresponding both to the variety of historical cultures and to forms of religious expression within any single tradition. There are even religions, like several forms of Buddhism, which do not depend on any notion of divinity. It is not difficult to conclude that there could be as many versions of religiousness as there are religious cultures. Religion appears as morality but also ecstasy, worship but also enlightenment, living in harmony with the earth but also being redeemed from a sinful world. To generalize about what religion "is" is difficult enough just on the ground of cross-cultural, historical study, completely apart from issues of philosophical or religious value judgments as to what it "ought" to be. We shall see later the extent to which even the cross-cultural study of religion participates in judgments of its own.

Configuring the World

While this book is about interpreting religion, we would first do well to think broadly about the wider role of interpretation in all experience. All perception, for example, may be said to have an interpretive, framing dimension.

All experience of the world is shaped by a process of selection. Every organism, as it reads its surroundings, responds to some objects and not to others, and experiences the world through a certain schema. The manner and sensory means by which living things construe their environment will be the same media through which the environment—"the world"—gives itself back to them. The world is full of objects we do not notice, either because we are not interested in them or because we are not equipped to see them. We only see what concerns us, those things for which we have a category. As an art historian puts it, "we only see what we look at."[8] Different kinds of animals perceive and respond to different kinds of objects—especially those useful for their survival. Self-interest and species-interest thus guide the way the world is both experientially configured and ignored. If a thing is not edible, if it is irrelevant to reproduction and territory (conceived either physically or conceptually), if it is not to be feared, it may as well not exist.

In this sense the world is always configured through a process of interpretation. There is no unmediated environment, no wholly innocent eye.[9] Whether perceptually or conceptually, whether in the physical world or in the world of ideas, to exist is to choose and to form one's environment, picking from a mass of potential material just those items that engage one's needs and interests. Sensing the world through its nose, a dog will "read" the events of a walk differently than its visually oriented human companion. On the same path, they will have been in different worlds. In this sense *environment*, and thus *world*, are highly relational terms. They are selections.

Language is a primary medium through which humans inhabit their world.[10] Language names what the world is, and the world complies, delivering itself back to us through our own namings. Languages are indeed like habitats, each culture building its value-orientations into its vocabularies. The perception of time, space, nature, and human relations will be intimately connected with one's terminology. Even within one culture there will be different kinds of specialized languages, such as science, religion, and the arts—all matrices that shape the world quite variously.

The difference between the world that comes to us through science and the world that comes to us through poetry and music is a difference between the media employed. The world forms itself around our symbols—whether they are impersonal scientific concepts, poetic metaphors, religious images, lines of music, or the movements of a dance. What lies outside such environments and outside our named objects (whether the objects are called electrons or spirits, viruses or demons) escapes our notice, and what rises up around our viewing lens becomes "the way things are."

This pluralistic, ecological image of *world* as a varying, interpretive matrix differs from the assumption that the world is flatly equivalent to that pictured by a single frame, whether that of biology, chemistry, physics, monotheism, Marxism, or Buddhism. Worlds are concomitants of such languages. To chemistry the world is made up of combinations of chemical elements; to physics, it is more basically made up of atomic matter and energy. Religion, on the other hand, posits images of existence which describe human consciousness as a participant in the world, picturing an inhabited universe in which moral and spiritual actions are factors in how life unfolds. The languages of science and religion, then, are not just conflicting representations of the same world, but organs of different worlds, in turn yielding different experiences of the environment—just as electronic equipment "sees" different objects than did Shakespeare.

The same person can alternately perceive the world scientifically, religiously, and poetically, without feeling that these are mutually exclusive, just as one can speak many languages and not feel that they contradict each other. The world can be seen in terms of hydrogen, in terms of beauty, or in terms of divinity. But the divinity lens will not reveal the chemical table of elements, and the electron microscope is not apt to produce a system of morality. And religions themselves differ. If biblical theologians see everywhere signs of a supreme being's creating and liberating activity, Buddhists will see the endless structurings and obstructions of enlightened awareness. Even the ordinary rounds of experience filter life through the discontinuous, heterogeneous media of sleep, dreams, sport, play, ceremony, music, theater, humor and laughter, love and sexuality, work and drudgery, conflict and peace.

Interpretation is not just the realm of nonscientific "opinions" as opposed to solid facts, not just an elitist, academic pastime, but the translation of what we observe into frames of meaning and thus part of the natural process of construing the world. It is present in the act of language itself. We play the creator every time we speak. We reshape the world every time we say what something means. And with this notion of the creation of meaning, we now come to the more specific nature of interpretation as a human activity.

Forms and Purposes of Interpretation

In the ordinary sense of the word, to *interpret* is to bring out the meaning of something that would not otherwise be clear.[11] The object could be a word, a text, or an action. It could be a period of history or it could be a gesture. But what does it mean to bring out the meaning of something? Why, in the realm of culture, do humans interpret?

Cultures have produced numerous special systems of interpreting the world. We have seen that languages themselves are such systems, and that sciences, mythologies, and philosophies of every kind function as specialized languages. They are the various ways of translating visible data from the world into a realm of meaning or significance. They deal with every area of life—from automobiles to military affairs to health to scriptures to electronics. When in doubt, we call in the experts who can "read" a particular set of evidence. Each religion, like each field of science, is a kind of training system for its own way of construing the world. Interpretation is then the reading of one kind of evidence or another in one fashion or another. It makes sense that different kinds of interpretation will be geared for different kinds of objects.

Interpretation can be simple or complex. At one level it is a matter of identifying objects and what they denote. For example, the term *aqua* can be interpreted in English as "water," and a musical notation may be read as "G-sharp." Yet the interpretation of *Don Quixote* or the performance of a Chopin Ballade is a larger undertaking, which requires more complex skills. Likewise, in religion, the image of a lotus may conventionally stand for purity, yet coming up with a framework for interpreting religion as a whole system of behavior and symbolism is an enormous task.

Each culture or area of cumulative interpretation has its agreed-upon systems of signs—with their meanings—and procedures for reading them. For example, it is social convention that determines whether an illness is to be interpreted through the "evidences" of witchcraft or of bacterial infection. In a traditional society where the practice of divination[12] is taken for granted, the lines of a sheep's liver may be read for their exact correspondences with certain kinds of fate or messages from the gods. Schools of biblical interpretation traditionally give students specific guidelines on how to understand the words of the Bible, criteria that conform to the doctrines of their tradition. Just as Catholics, Protestants, and Jews are taught to read the scripture in ways that illustrate their own beliefs, so Freudians and Jungians are trained to read dreams in ways that illustrate their respective principles.

Evidence, then, is indeed ultimately relative to the communal models which define it, and the meaning of religion will be determined by which school of thought the interpreter represents.

Causes versus Meanings. Sometimes *interpretation* is connected with scientific programs of causal explanation; usually, however, it is associated with the humanistic explication of meanings. These are quite different tasks. Some would even reserve the term *explanation* for science and *interpretation* for humanistic topics.

The first approach is often linked with the goal of determining what produces a phenomenon—with uncovering its origins or antecedent conditions. It is part of the spirit of science to ask *why*—why the planets move in elliptical orbit or why this bridge collapsed rather than that one. In the same way, there are schools of interpretation that trace religion back to certain emotions, social conditions, cultural needs, ignorant beliefs, and so on. These are then shown to be the material out of which religion is made.

Yet while causal explanation is the foundation of science, it has limitations with regard to accounting for the subject matter of religion. The aspects of religion that can be objectively explained by verifiable causes or conditions are often the least interesting (and least religious) parts of the subject matter. A Beethoven string quartet is at one level "caused" by the rubbing of a horsehair bow against catgut or metal strings. A cathedral is "produced" by an assemblage of stones and bricks. The antecedent condition of every human act is an activity of neurons. All religious life is influenced by social contexts. Do these fully explain the quartet, the cathedral, falling in love, or religious experience; or do they just explain preconditions of these phenomena? While such explanations may themselves have meanings in the world of the explainer, they are clearly a different kind of interpretive approach from one which tries to show what religious objects signify *to people* or even what they signify religiously.

At the other end of the spectrum from explaining an object by its causes is the process of expounding its meanings. The question here is not where a religious expression comes from, but what it symbolizes. Indeed, a central, historical use of the word *interpretation* in religion is the exegesis (literally, "to lead or guide out") of scriptural texts. [13] What does the serpent in the Garden of Eden signify? What is the meaning of the Tree of Life? What is the significance of Christ's Incarnation? Even in asking the meteorological question, "What do those clouds in the sky signify?" we want to know not just about causes, but what the clouds *refer to*. It is the same with the "meaning" of a religious symbol or text, or for that matter of an enigmatic remark. Most of the approaches we will examine are in effect systems for showing that religious expressions are about some order of reality other than what is apparent on the surface.

While the words *explanation* and *interpretation* are often used synonymously in popular speech, in scientific contexts the first is more typically understood to be grounded in testable, empirical analysis. At the same time, the possibility of rigorous, analytical theory-making as applied to religion is currently under much review. [14]

Meaning—to Whom? Talk about the "meaning" of religion often fails to be clear about this exceedingly important question. For meaning always implies meaning *to someone*. There is no meaning in general or in objects by themselves. Meaning is not a vague, rootless substance floating in the air or intrinsically embedded in the world, but the significance of an object to a specific culture or person.

When we look at religion, do we look at what it means to adherents or at what it means within the bounds of our own theory?

In certain approaches to religion the concept of *understanding* has come to play a central role, even to the point where some would fuse interpretation and understanding. [15] A host of interesting issues surrounds the question of what it means to really understand something religious. Some have even argued that to understand religion requires being religious. If you understand mysticism, one observer even wrote, then you are a mystic.

Yet many theories of religion see themselves as alternatives to religion's view of itself, and are only interested in what religion means within their own explanatory system. The object, religion, is here brought into one's own territory of meaning, and whatever it means to the insider is irrelevant.

Evidence and Imagination. At one extreme, interpretation is meaning based on conventional evidence. There are guidelines to follow, misinterpretations to avoid. We stick to ordinary rules of evidence in figuring out who or what broke the kitchen jar, as does a detective in construing the circumstances of a crime, or a radiologist in reading X rays for the presence or absence of disease, or an archeologist in determining the historical period of artifacts.

At the other extreme are types of creative interpretation where the meaning of an object is imaginatively superimposed by the interpreter without regard to contrary evidence. Anyone is free to interpret water as a symbol in any way they wish, no matter how whimsically or for what purpose. Any object can be seen in a thousand and one ways, and the same event can be retold by eyewitnesses in quite dissimilar versions. The interpreter here places meanings on objects in order to see those objects through his or her own associations. If these meanings are not connected with an interpretive community that has orthodox ways to read the objects, we would call this *imaginative* interpretation. It is a category that includes both creative geniuses and paranoid schizophrenics. A caricature drawing, for example, is an imaginative interpretation. It may be brilliantly insightful in spite of its exaggerations. But an interpretation it surely is, and no one would ask whether it was empirically proven or not. An actor's portrayal of a role or a violinist's performance of a composition are also examples of imaginative, performatory interpretations. So in interpretation there are both scientific and artistic models.

Interpretation as a Form of Behavior. Interpretations of religion are not just pure intellectual activity, but also a kind of social behavior, motivated social acts. As with language generally, it typically involves a kind of "politics," insofar as it is an act conditioned by the assertive or defensive role that one's interpretive stance plays in society. Interpretation can be used to attack, dispute, correct, or dismiss. It can be conciliating or provocative, diplomatic or audacious, triumphantly self-elevating or resentfully cynical. It maintains established positions and it overthrows them, often as a counterinterpretation to another one which seems threatening, shallow, or embarrassing. Sometimes it takes to the streets; sometimes it is modest and self-deprecating. Over words of interpretation (are we invaders or are we liberators?) wars are waged, people are ostracized, tortured, and executed, nations and lives are destroyed. Well known are the battles for interpretive supremacy between evolutionism and creationism, Marxism and capitalism, Catholicism and Protestantism.

Of every interpretation of religion, then, we will ask what it is trying to accomplish, and we will situate it in the contexts which give it its own intelligibility and method.

Overview

The following chapters aim to concisely present some major ways of interpreting religious life, and to show the way these frames expose different aspects of the subject. While no attempt is made to survey the entire range of modern theories of religion, a representative diversity is included.

We begin with major critical views on religion, as these pose the issue of interpretation in dramatic form (chapter 2). For example, in the critiques of Marx and Freud, religion is of strictly human origin and illusory, and its real social function is not at all what religious people think it is.

We then turn to three major, different contexts into which religion is typically "translated" by those who have taken it seriously as a subject matter for modern analysis. The first framework is that of social anthropology, which sees religion as an expression of varying sociocultural values (chapter 3). The second framework is depth psychology, which views religious symbols as expressions of the life and development of the psyche (chapter 4). The third is that of comparative religion, which sees particular religious phenomena as expressions of cross-cultural religious patterns and types (chapter 5). Each of these frameworks has evolved its own vocabulary for describing what religion is about, and each has an applicability and force of its own.

But insiders, too, interpret religion (chapter 6). We will look at ways that different religious philosophies—whether in narrow or in broad, universalistic terms—explain the diversity of religion

and make their own distinctions between levels of religious understanding. Because they are parts of the phenomenon of interpretation, inside views on religion are included alongside those of
critics and social scientists, without giving any of them a privileged or disprivileged position.

The last chapters (7–8) present ways of understanding the
variety of interpretation, primarily by showing its unavoidably
contextual nature. They advocate a pluralistic capability that
could negotiate different angles on religion. A positive, dynamic
notion of relativity emerges here, which recognizes the inevitable
connection between the stance of the interpreter and the facets of
religion that come into view.

2

The Challenge: Critical
Interpretations of Religion

What religion interprets as God, its critics interpret as illusion. What religion interprets as holy scripture, critics interpret as human fabrication. What religion interprets as divinely ordained traditions, critics interpret as systems of repression and domination. What religion interprets as freedom, critics interpret as false security.

The issue of interpretation is given an acute, dramatic form in the voices of critics. They show how incisive a force is the interpretive lens, when what for centuries was taken as eternal truth can in a day become insidious fiction. At the blink of an interpretive eye the sacred becomes ordinary, divine authority becomes despotism, and the absolute becomes relative. One universe vanishes and another replaces it. The gods are unmasked, and the terms of the world are utterly reversed.

In order to sense some of the range of what is at stake in interpretation, we begin with the major critical views on religion.

While all new theory by its very nature is a countertheory to a ruling view, challenging the boundaries that maintained some previous domain, in the case of religion the boundaries have been especially sacrosanct and the stakes especially high. In times of strong religious authority, unacceptable readings of the scripture were no trivial matter. Atheists and philosophical heretics were not just sources of error—they were horrors and abominations. In many cases religious institutions resisted the ideological subver-

sion of their world with ferocity—by excommunications and in-
quisitions, torture and death sentences. For construing God as an
"ineffable One" rather than as a Trinity, the Unitarian Michael
Servetus was burned at the stake in John Calvin's Geneva. It is a
mark of the profound territorial and authoritarian nature of traditional, dogmatic interpretations of religion that the history of
counterinterpretations of religion has been so limned with blood.

By the late eighteenth century, however, European culture
was itself beginning to make a transition to secular modernity and
some of the attendant values of scientific investigation and social
tolerance, and issues of religion came to be resolved less at the
stake than in books. But a different breed of nonconformists was
emerging; not just deviant theologians, but a whole succession of
critics of the very concept of religion. A modern era of nonreligious interpretation rose up to challenge religion in various
lines of attack. The gods that were the base of civilizations were
now demystified wholesale; and religion was viewed at best as folly
and error and at worst as a malignant form of oppression.

Rationalism: Religion as Primitive Thought

Since the eighteenth century the most common nonreligious
framework for explaining religion has been that of rationalism.[1]
Rationalism is the characteristic criterion of the age of science or
the "Age of Enlightenment," in which we still supposedly live. It
is an attempt to replace supernatural thinking with naturalistic
thinking, maintaining that reason is the only valid source of
knowledge about the world. In many ways this has become a
modern worldview, ensconced in public educational systems. Religion—with its associations of revelation and miracles—is perceived as outside the realm of this system of knowledge, and is
accordingly relegated to the separate, self-contained domains of
churches, homes, and individual practice. As religions had once
banned the study of atheistic writings, secular countries now
banned the teaching of religion in public schools.

In the rationalist view, supernatural beliefs are unscientific
and unfounded, products of primitive, pre-critical thinking. Religion here represents the childhood of thought, a kind of organized
fairy tale, humanity's early attempt to conceive and explain the
unknown and the fearful, awesome forces of nature, life, and
death. In this framework, religion is a mentality untutored by

rational criteria, knowing no boundary between fact and imagination. Rationalism sees religious explanation as its own polar opposite.

To a rationalist the world seems to subsist very well on its own, without any need for the hypothesis of a creator god or spiritual agencies. All events are explainable as acts of nature, with no need to appeal to myth or divine intervention. The physical sciences first dismantled the biblical view of the outer world, and then the human sciences undermined the religious image of human nature itself—now to be conceived in terms of behavior patterns and brain physiology rather than soul.

Rationalism has had various incarnations, depending on historical settings and needs. For example, in seventeenth- and eighteenth-century France and England, Deism was in fashion. This philosophy was a kind of half-way house between religion and science. Deists challenged what they took to be narrow-minded beliefs in miracles and supernatural explanations, while still maintaining confidence in a higher principle of order in the universe, namely God (hence the name Deism)—because after all, this itself was an affirmation that was to them reasonable.

The Scottish philosopher David Hume (1711–76) was perhaps rationalism's pivotal figure in the systematic nature of his arguments against religious claims for theism and revelation, in his view that religion arises due to ignorant, mistaken inferences about true causes, and in his advocacy for a complete "science of man." His philosophical influence, with its explicit refusal to privilege any part of religious thought, was far-reaching and has extended to the present.

In the late nineteenth century, evolutionism became another rationalist framework for interpreting the development of religious thought. After Darwin's *The Origin of Species* (1859) religious ideas could now confidently and explicitly be traced to early, "primitive" societies. Anthropology, then a new science based on the study of tribal cultures and the reconstruction of human beginnings, provided numerous theories and speculations about the origins of religion in the workings of archaic mentality. For example, the famous animism theory set forth by Edward B. Tylor in 1871 hypothesized that religion begins with the belief in souls and spirits, a belief that arose from the need to explain the appearance of animated figures in dream states and the difference between the living body and the corpse. The belief in gods is but a later elaboration of this premise. Still other theories explained the origin of the religious sentiment in feelings of the impressiveness of nature—as in the activity of the heavenly bodies or the cyclical life-death processes of the earth—showing that early humans ignorantly attributed spiritual agency to these forces. James G. Frazer's theory was typical of the period: that people first related to the world through the mentality of magic, then through religious propitiation (when magic failed to be dependable), and ultimately through science.[2]

Positivism, another form of rationalism, was a philosophical movement emphasizing that only what is verifiable by scientific method, that is, falsifiable, can produce real knowledge. As the presence of the supernatural cannot be proved or disproved by any form of observation, it has no claim to truth. For example, if one claims that God is the creator and maintainer of the world, but there is no evidence that could possibly *disconfirm* this assertion, the belief must be empty and noncognitive.

The Human versus Divine Origins of Religion

If the rationalist critique saw religion as a mistaken form of explanation, another line of criticism showed how religion is made out of human needs and projections; it is an invention constructed of our own psychological and social symbols and experience. To explain religion in this way is to show not just that it is an error of the mind, but to uncover its actual generative source in human nature. "The divine" is not just a mistake, but a disguised symbol of human power and feeling.

There is no question here of holding out for a higher, more reasonable form of God: the very concept of a divine order becomes a human construct. This new frame, which began in the middle of the nineteenth century and was epitomized by Friedrich Nietzsche's announcement of the great cultural event of "the death of God"[3]—and the subsequent transfer of power to humanity—we now examine.

Religion as an Expression of Social Alienation. The publication in 1841 of Ludwig Feuerbach's *The Essence of Christianity* gave philosophic expression to the idea that God and religion are projections of humanity.[4] For Feuerbach religion is not "the divine" realizing itself in humanity, as with previous idealistic philosophies, but instead humanity's own realization of *itself*. It is a characteristic of human nature to know itself through objectifications. God, for example, is a projection of our own self-consciousness, imagined in its pure form and made of the human qualities of power, wisdom, and love. Religion is our dream, a mirror of our true nature. But because we put everything holy into the Supreme Being, this makes us weak, servile beings, the opposite of the ideal god. Feuerbach's solution was to espouse a religion that explicitly made humanity its object—that reintegrated into human realization what had been split off as a divine projection.

These ideas had a direct influence on the young Karl Marx.[5] Marx extended the idea that religion is humanly "produced" by showing its specific origin in social and economic conflicts and needs. He saw all human consciousness as based on collective forces, and as a mirror of evolving social history and order. Religion is generated from social powerlessness but can become a strategy of social control. Because the dominant ideas of a society are the ideas of its ruling class, religious ideology is maintained by power and status, and "God" becomes a status-enhancing, manipulative symbol of such authority.

Religion arises out of the need for a better world than the social conditions of life offer. It is an imagined solution to the despair over those conditions, a refuge from a world of troubles. In Marx's famous words, "Religion is the sigh of the oppressed creature, the heart of a heartless world, just as it is the spirit of a spiritless situation. It is the opium of the people."[6] Religion is thus an inverted, duplicate world mirroring in reverse the human condition—an imaginary other realm in which we seek solace and compensation for our trials on earth.

Because religious beliefs are made of the stuff of human alienation, they will disappear when life on earth becomes livable and harmonious. Marxists claim that they themselves, and not the religionists, are the ones creating the real "kingdom" of justice here below, that they are the real "good Samaritans" treating the afflicted. Religion is a symptom of an illness that will be cured, when people are no longer forced to dream of other worlds to give themselves dignity, and can instead establish the conditions of dignity in actual historical societies. Marx wrote: "The abolition of religion as the *illusory* happiness of the people is required for their *real* happiness. The demand to give up the illusion about its condition is the *demand to give up a condition which needs illusions.*

The criticism of religion is therefore *in embryo the criticism of the vale of woe,* the *halo* of which is religion."[7]

So religious projections are not just mental errors or mistakes in reasoning, but compensatory symptoms and statements about very specific social realities. The Marxist looks to social "self-cleavage" to see the roots of our projections, ultimately construing that cleavage to lie in the presence of an exploiting class. The exploited are the alienated, and their religious distress is "at the same the *expression* of real distress and the *protest* against real distress."[8] The great imaginary universes of religion compensate in heaven our homelessness on earth, and keeping the peasantry dependent on this subjection is the function of the ruling class. To Marx this meant the creation of "false consciousness"—where ideas reflect only the self-interest of the dominant segments of society.

Today, versions of the Marxist approach are numerous and intellectually pervasive, maintaining in one way or another that religion is the camouflage of social power.

Religion as a Projection of Unconscious Relationships. Sigmund Freud (1856–1939) also saw religion as a projection of human wishes,[9] but explained this in terms of his general theory of unconscious sublimation. The Freudian approach, with its many variations and developments, also remains an influential model for explaining religion and culture.[10]

Archrationalist and trained neurologist, Freud faced centuries of prescientific ideas about the mind, and courageously determined to replace these with a new theory that featured the discovery of an unconscious part of the psyche.[11] His paradigm represented a new possibility in the history of interpretation: the concept that there are unconscious psychological motivations which produce and maintain religious symbols.

In Freud's view, our deepest psychological motivations reflect emotional relationships—the ways we attempt to either avoid or come to terms with dependencies and traumas experienced in our ego development. The human ego is a fragile affair beset on all sides by repressed, emotion-laden material from its past. Religions are the collective neuroses and dreams that allow us to express and reenact such unconscious contents. Freud was not just repeating the old Greek view that we make gods in our own image (or as the ancient philosopher Xenophanes put it, if horses and oxen could draw, they would draw gods that looked like horses and oxen). He was saying more: that our strong relationships to gods represent actual relationships to parental images; i.e., that the perception of gods in terms of love, fear, and punishment reflects the ambivalence of the ego's relation to its earliest surrounding authorities. The parental relationship—epitomized in the Oedipus complex—springs "from the biological fact of the long helplessness and slow maturing of the young human being, and the complicated development of his capacity for love."[12]

Through its gods and mythologies, religion symbolizes or "substitutes" representations of our ego's relationships to its original emotional ties and fears. Gods supply the feeling of being accepted, the exposure of guilt and its expiatory resolution, the lost strength and protective authority of the father, and the sense that one's sacrifices are viewed favorably and rewarded. We experience oneness with the divine as a way of regressing to a pre-egoic, boundary-less state of security known in infancy or even the womb. Mythic gardens of paradise reiterate uterine utopias. Rites of communion administered by robed priests and "mother Church" activate the self's original alimentary dependency on the nurturing biological mother. In religion we "come home."

Thus religion's appeal is in the compelling, potent strength of its symbols to cathect or resolve ego needs. The often obsessional nature of religious practice arises because of the emotional strength of repressed parts of our psyche, material that reaches our consciousness only through symbols which conceal their function.

According to Freud, religion addresses sexual needs in this concealed way. Mystical experience of ecstasy, the mystic's "intimate union of I and Thou," or "infusion of the soul with the rapture of the divine"—are really self-produced unconscious surrogates for sexual expression. Possession cults often legitimize orgasmic behavior under the guise that it is the activity of the possessing spirit. Monks and nuns, unconnected with worldly love, wed themselves to Christ. Scenarios of the body of Christ—stretched on the cross, pierced with nails, cared for by women—or of the mother of god holding the divine male infant in her lap or at her breast, all express and satisfy facets of the believer's own sexuality. Asceticism, on the other hand, with its mortification of the flesh, acts out the cultural repression and sublimation of sexual desire and its accompanying guilt. Religious life becomes a disguised code for emotional satisfactions which ordinary social roles inhibit.

Religious doctrines like "eternal life and its rewards" Freud called illusions, that is, thoughts created by wishes—wishes in this case that answer our needs for consolation and justification. We unconsciously picture the world the way we desire it to be. But for all its wishful thinking, religion to Freudians is ultimately less the way we come to terms with our future, and more the way we relive our past.

As with Marxism, Freudian interpretation is not just philosophical, but has a practical application: to free society and the individual psyche from the inhuman repressiveness of religious ideas. The analysis of religion is not performed as a purely theoretical or scientific activity, but as an act of liberation, as with the Marxist slogan that the purpose of philosophy is not just to interpret the world but to change it. The critique of ruling class oppression, wrote Marx, "is criticism in a *hand-to-hand fight,* and in such a fight the point is not whether the opponent is a nobler, equal, *interesting* opponent, the point is to *strike* him."[13] "The criticism of religion," he continued, "ends with the teaching that *man is the highest essence for man,* hence with the categoric imperative to overthrow all relations in which man is a debased, enslaved, abandoned, despicable essence."[14] Likewise, in the setting of psychoanalytic work, Freud perceived religion as the enemy of free thought and as a guilt-producing factor in the formation of individual psychopathologies. The object of therapy is for the ego to become conscious of what is repressed, so as not to be prone to irrational or defensive behavior. We cannot be fully conscious until we are aware of our hitherto unconscious wishes and projections. We cannot cure society if we do not know the disease.

Scripture as a Product of Human History

Another form of erosion of religious claims came on historical grounds. By the end of the eighteenth century, critical methods of analyzing scripture were emerging, calling into question its divine status.

To Westerners, the Holy Bible had been not only the anchor of religion but the premise and framework of all historical understanding. It was placed on a completely different level than any other book, in a privileged category by itself. It was assumed to be a faithful account of the world and self-evident proof of the supremacy of biblical religion. Other peoples' religious texts were only "mythologies" and acts of human imagination.

When, throughout the nineteenth century and into the twentieth, scholars began to demonstrate that biblical texts could be analyzed by the same standards as any piece of writing, and that their contents could be explained as human compositions, the foundations of religion were shaken in yet another way. What for ages had been taken as divinely revealed seemed now to be one more product of human history, fashioned out of the needs of evolving social contexts. The words of God became the words of ancient editors. The miracles of the Bible, traditionally understood as astonishing signs of divine sponsorship, were no longer accepted at face value but interpreted either as literary embellishments or as reportage of naturalistic phenomena misinterpreted as supernatural (for example, what caused the Red Sea to part for Moses was not an intervening act of God but a tidal phenomenon). For many, the presence in the Bible of conflicting styles and vocabularies, repetitions and editorial additions, the use of different names for the deity, and incongruous historical references pointed to a work of human rather than divine hands. Discovery of Babylonian mythologies and of writings by other inhabitants of Palestine during the biblical period also showed that the scriptural accounts were influenced by religious ideas of these particular environments.

In this critical approach, the all-important first five books of the Bible, the writings traditionally ascribed to Moses, appeared to not be handed down by divine inspiration, but were rather the result of many authors writing from the viewpoints of different centuries with different kinds of religious and political agendas. According to this "documentary hypothesis,"[15] for example, there is little in these books (Genesis, Exodus, Leviticus, Numbers, and Deuteronomy) that could have been written at the actual time of Moses (thirteenth century B.C.E.). Most of the laws were written by a priestly class well after the Babylonian exile (586 B.C.E.), and most of Deuteronomy (consisting largely of discourses assigned to Moses) also gives evidence of having been composed several hundred years *after* Moses and piously inserted back into his time in order to give it more sacred authority.

New Testament gospels also came to be read by historical critics[16] not as eyewitness accounts but as expressions of the ideals and faith of the early Christian community—in a sense, as pious propaganda designed to prove to readers and converts the divinity and messiahship of Jesus. Events in the life of Jesus were seen to have been "created" as literary tableaux in order to conform to Hebrew prophecies—whereas the faithful Christian insider had always read these as the miraculous fulfillments of what had been predicted centuries before. The Gospel of John was construed not as the direct report of a contemporary disciple but as a much later spiritual interpretation of Christ, drawing on the imagery of Hellenistic redeemer mythologies and putting mystical sayings in the mouth of Jesus—as the creators of the heretical Gnostic gospels were also to do in the second century C.E.

Historicism, the view that cultural traditions and values should be studied as products of history and historical context, remains an ongoing influence in religious and biblical studies, in spite of Fundamentalist repudiations of it, and its influence has not been limited to Western traditions.

The Negative Functions of Religion

Some challenges to religion are based not on theories of origin but on criticism of the consequences of religion for society. The dysfunctional effects of religion then imply the self-evident end of its claims to truth. If the fruits are bad, the tree is bad. No theoretical apparatus—for example, historical materialism or the psychology of the unconscious—is even needed, since religion is patently condemned by its own behavior. In the Greco-Roman world philosophers often criticized and ridiculed religion on the basis of the immoral, capricious, and vindictive behavior of the gods themselves. Religion's "crimes against life" were a strong point in the Marxist, Nietzschean, and Freudian attacks; and to many ordinary observers its coercive, authoritarian elements are religion's dominant features.

We have already seen how for Marx religion is a force of social compulsion, repression, and oppression. Religion is part of the false authority of the empowered classes, which justifies their own power and status and maintains their social structure and hierarchy against social change and justice. It is a spell cast over society to hold people in the thrall of its own political values, encoding archaic social stratifications in doctrines of supposed cosmic truth. Marxists thus point to the reactionary role religion has historically played in maintaining class and caste divisions and in legitimating racial and nationalistic superiority and imperialism. During the United States Civil War, for example, Southerners devoutly cited passages from the Bible as evidence of God's ordination of the institution of black slavery.

A variant on the interpretation of religion as camouflaged social tyranny is the feminist criticism of patriarchal, sexist scriptures and theologies.[17] Where the world is pictured in terms of the supremacy of male roles, male heroes, male gods, and the male values of power, hierarchy, territory, violence, and rulership, religion blindly perpetuates one-sided values. It subordinates women and chauvinistically belittles or excludes their spiritual roles and modes of spiritual experience.

Religion, another related argument runs, is also intellectually repressive. It prevents, inhibits, and enslaves truth and thought by subordinating them to dogma. It disallows anything in science and history that doesn't fit its doctrines and laws; refusing, as in the case of Galileo, to look through the telescope. By clinging to ancient worldviews, religion closes its eyes to new forms of thought and life.

Finally, there are those to whom religion is simply not religious. Instead of embodying peace and love, it acts out divisiveness, intolerance, and fanaticism. The term religion here conjures up catastrophic crusades and holy wars past and present, conflicts that put "the will of God" on one's own side, Satan on the other. Religion thereby makes a foul coalescence of holiness and self-interest, a demonic alliance of mythology and social prejudice.

In such ways, by the criterion that there is no difference between what someone is and what someone does, the validity of religion is judged by its effects on society and found wanting. In a parallel way, some have thought that the most telling refutation of the existence of a good and all-powerful god is the existence of a world of brutality and evil. The argument against religion here is the existence of the world itself.

Assessment

The traditional interpreter, religion, has here become the interpreted. That which was once beyond criticism here becomes the object of full attack. In this age of suspicion,[18] the tables are turned, as the voices of the critics represent modern culture's own processes of self-doubt and self-scrutiny. Religion, it seems, is not what it says it is after all. It is a masked human construct. Society made it and maintains it.

There is a distinctly retortive nature to many of these criticisms.[19] They arise as a response to perceived abuses. They are replies to felt oppression. Many of them show that the interpreter's world has been offended by the liabilities of a religious era, which require pointed counterattack. They represent a spectrum of counteraccusations corresponding to a spectrum of religious threats.

Each critique focuses on an aspect of religion that threatens the critique's own values and position. Thus rationalism attacks what looks nonrational, social criticism focuses on what looks antisocial, Freudian criticism is leveled at what looks psychologically obstructive, and historical criticism of the Bible is directed at what looks like historical falsifications that contradict evidence. Critics of various kinds see what they dislike about religion and typically take those traits as the basis for defining the entire nature of religion.

Yet the above criticisms of religion are for the most part viewpoints that are themselves historically situated responses to certain historically situated forms of Western religion. Several assume *religion* to be equivalent to the one the critics are familiar with, that of Western society. In fact, by modern, cross-cultural standards, some of them are not really theories of religion at all, but counterestablishment reactions to certain forms of biblical monotheism. Generalizations with any claim to be inclusive would need to consider *all* forms of religion. For example, there are types of religious life which are explicitly nonviolent, intended to transcend rather than affirm social roles; nonsexist or goddess-oriented; aimed at overcoming unconscious projections rather than indulging in them; or geared to serving and liberating rather than ruling the poor. Many religious people would therefore say that what these critics call religion is not real religion at all.

Sometimes counterexplanations seem to have a specifically defensive character, as when people become suspicious of new religious movements or sects and without any particular investigation automatically explain them in nonreligious terms. Has someone converted? It must be due to loneliness or brainwashing. For to accept the convertee's own religious explanation might seem tantamount to accepting the existence or viability of a religious realm that in turn challenges one's own worldview.

In several of the above critiques the assertion that religion is "only" social, psychological, historical, or human is a way of denying the supernatural claims of monotheism. That is, the positing of a "human" side is part of a paired opposition ("the human" vs. "the divine"), and makes sense only within the contrast. Yet this dichotomy would have less relevance in nondualistic Asian religions, where the human and the divine are not conceived to be opposites. Moreover, if the claim that religion is "only" human makes a certain point in the context of Western religious dualisms which assert a division of supernatural and natural realms, the term "human" and its analogues ("social," "psychological," "natural," etc.) remain more open-ended and philosophically ambiguous if they stand on their own rather than in contrast to "the supernatural." For what, after all, is human? The limits of what is human are not known in any agreed-upon way. While critical views of religion appear to explain the unknown in terms of the nonmysterious known (the human), ultimately the known becomes another unknown. Moreover, if something originates in the psyche, or in society, or in history, does that in itself mean that it is fictional? Are scientific concepts fictional because they are "only made by humans?" What is *not* illusion? What ideology is not related to changing models of social authority?

Even without the denunciatory emphasis of the critical views, the concept of the human matrix and explanation of religion has remained a postulate of the modern social sciences, and many religious studies scholars today also generally acknowledge the important role of sociological and psychological factors in forming their subject matter. The question, then, is less *whether* religious forms correlate with forms of cultural and historical setting, and more *how* to interpret this. *Context*, we shall see, is a term that can be used in different ways and uttered with different overtones— each summoning a different interpretive mood and frame.

A major frame of interpretation is the sociological one. Apart from its role in challenging religious thought, the sociocultural model for explaining religion—the subject of the next chapter— became far-ranging, thorough, and powerful in its application and deserves a forum of its own. No theory of religion, and no treatment of interpretations of religion, can disregard its comprehensive point of view.

3

As Society, So Religion

The study of religion as a social phenomenon has gone well beyond Marx and his accusatory critique. It has become a broad, widely accepted framework in the modern social sciences.[1] The sociology and anthropology of religion are founded on the affirmations that the differences between kinds of religion are explainable in terms of the differences between kinds of societies, and that the ingredients of religion are ultimately the projected or encoded values of society and culture. In what I will present here as the sociocultural approach, every aspect of religion is systematically shown to be an expression of collective life. Once religion is taken out of the domain of the supernatural, it is not difficult for a secular world to conclude that it is lock, stock, and barrel a creation of human society.

The social theory of religion in its deepest impact is not just about the mechanics of how society *influences* religion, (e.g., as in the extent to which social class affects church affiliation), but about the very origin of religion as a social construction. Religion is seen as an expression of collective values rather than as an expression of divine revelation. Gods, moral codes, and the distinction of sacred and profane are here understood as the products and instruments of culture.

This chapter outlines and illustrates the rationale by which all forms of religious life can be viewed as social phenomena.

Society: The Source of Religion

In 1912 the French sociologist Emile Durkheim published what was to become the classic theory of the sociology of religion, *The Elementary Forms of the Religious Life.* [2] It remains the best-known manifesto of the sociological position, and indispensable reading for every student of religion.

Durkheim faced two ways of explaining religion that he considered inadequate. The first option was theological, explaining religion in terms of its own supernatural categories; and the second was materialistic and rationalistic, explaining religion as an illusion of the senses and imagination. The first approach seemed to be outside the bounds of scientific observation, and the second seemed to dismiss religion as essentially unworthy of study. But Durkheim thought that religion was too powerful a form of culture either to put beyond the scope of science or to disregard. Over and against these options Durkheim proposed his famous third explanation.

This model was based on the concept of *society,* which Durkheim broadly conceived as a creative matrix of collective values. Religion here is neither something the stork brought nor a mere hallucination, but an expression of this very real system of power, authority, and meaning. To Durkheim this was an impartial, dispassionate middle ground and "a new way to the science of man." Religion was seen neither as having been revealed from outside of nature nor as a mistake in human reasoning to be thrown on the dust heap of history, but as a system of belief and behavior which represented social ideals.

Society was Durkheim's name for the systems of collective forces which have produced civilizations; schemas of science and knowledge; language; morality; and classifications of time, space, and causality. For Durkheim, *society* is the canopy of moral and conceptual categories, ideals, and sentiments which exists prior to individual experience. As children, individuals begin to participate in a language they did not themselves create, in a society that gives them the lenses through which the world takes on shape and symbolic meaning. Each society creates a culture, building its own inhabitable world.

Note that our colloquial use of the words *society* and *social* is narrower than the Durkheimian one. Modern individuals tend to see society as a kind of neutral backdrop to their activities, but to sociologists it is what creates the very nature of individual life, and is like a superorganism with a life and agency of its own.

In this theory, it is society that creates our roles and identities. If one can become a wandering monk, independent artist, or great, self-generated individualist it is because society has allowed or empowered these categories of behavior. Images of soul and selfhood are collective creations, as is the definition of saints and sinners. Society provides the scenarios within which its members act out their lives. Without a sense of social role—whether supported by clans, families, churches, peers, or even ancestral exemplars—individuals wither, as it were, for lack of a vine. Take away the audience and there can be no charismatic leader; take away the disciples and there can be no guru; without subjects there are no kings; without children there are no fathers or mothers.

Society in this usage becomes the explanatory master key to unlocking the mystery of how religion originated. If society creates civilization and all its sciences, cosmologies, and arts, it is not difficult to imagine that society has also created the gods. Science and religion, though they employ contrasting types of language, are both parts of the world-forming activity of collective life.

Religion, the Sacred, and the Totemic Principle. Durkheim found the origin of religion in the bonds that are formed with the sacred symbols of one's own group. His case study was the tribal religion of the Australian aboriginals, which he presumed represented the earliest form of human society. He saw here that each of over four hundred communities had its own distinct religious system centering around its own particular sacred ancestors. In the fact of this coexistence of different, equally sacred systems side by side, each with its own mythic history and ancestry, Durkheim saw a primal expression of the principle that each society constructs religion around its own horizon.

Following late nineteenth-century terminology, Durkheim used the concept of *totemism* to explain the origin of this principle of bonding with sacred objects. A *totem* is an animal or plant ancestor with whom a group like a clan believes itself to be spiritually kin. It becomes the mark or flag of the group's own existence and tradition. Durkheim noticed that each of the aboriginal clans not only had their own totemic species, but, more importantly, that the emblems of those species were the most sacred things in the society. A species was sacred not because of its intrinsic qualities—which were often quite humble and modest, like those of certain insect totems—but because of its symbolic function in signifying the identity of the tribe. The totems typically were represented in abstract designs on certain oblong boards known as *churingas*.

These holy objects (and there was nothing in tribal life more revered) Durkheim saw as concretizations and embodiments of a force that was real and powerful because it was charged with the very identity of the group itself. He called this force "the totemic principle." The intensity of sacred things derives from the intensity of this collective identity and the sanctity of its traditions. The gods and ancestors, after all, are *our* gods and ancestors, and faith is "the faith of our fathers." Thus for Durkheim, religious symbols and social symbols are ultimately the same thing.

Sacredness, which Durkheim took as a universal feature of all religious phenomena, is in this interpretation a value placed on objects by groups. This value can be expressed negatively through taboos and restrictions or positively through the purification requirements for solemn rites of communion with the sacred. But it is society that makes things sacred or profane, and every traditional society has sacred objects, persons, places, or times. To Durkheim, rationalist theories which maintain that religion originates in a prescientific attempt to explain the world of nature could not account for the absolute centrality of these institutions, i.e., the strong character of sacred-profane distinctions within a society. As a value placed on objects by the community, sacredness could be fully explained only in sociological terms.

In the Durkheimian perspective, the concept that communities condense their spiritual life into group-specific, focal symbols is not applicable only on the tribal level but also to the patron deities or saints of villages, the patron gods of city-states, and the holiness of objects like the Qur'an, the Torah, Christ, and Buddha within their respective traditions. In every case certain objects become laden with value placed on them by the group, whereas for those outside the circle of the community they are not sacred at all. Their holiness is relative to the community they serve. If Buddhists "take refuge in the Buddha, the Teachings, and the Community," Christians seek membership in Christ and His Church, Jews are at home in the Torah recorded by Moses, and Muslims submit to the Holy Qur'an as revealed through the Prophet Muhammed.

The history of religion is here read as the history of objects and observances made sacred by groups. Even secular societies give sacred focus to principles like equality, freedom, and democracy, embodying these ideas in revered constitutions, laws, and visual symbols.

In these ways sociology explains the existence of multiple systems of sacred things, and Durkheim was led to his characterization of religion as a system of beliefs and practices relative to sacred things, uniting into a moral community those who adhere to them.

The Religious Function of Society. The Durkheimians attributed to society the powers traditionally attributed to divinity. Indeed, they had a respect for the power of society analogous in some ways to believers' respect for religion and God. Like a creator god, society fashions the world and its sacred institutions, even affixing hallowed times and places. Like a lawgiver and moral guardian, society ordains the behavioral order of things and punishes violations. Society, like God, stands over and above all individuals, in power, enormity, authority, and sometimes grandeur. It consecrates leaders and destroys enemies. It requires sacrifice, dedication, and subordination on the part of its members, but is also the source of empowerment and enthusiasm. All that we know about obligation, loyalty, respect, and hierarchic behavior is learned in society, and our relationship to religious symbols simply mirrors those social relationships. Like a god, society gives to us and expects to receive back from us. Religious behavior really *is* social behavior.

A society is a system of order, the opposite of which is chaos.[3] Maintaining this order becomes one of its most important functions. This is why to some extent we fear chaos and the violation of order more than we love the gods. We often perform religious observances because we will not risk *not* doing so. To not be in the family pew on the Sabbath, to not eat fish rather than meat on Friday, to not perform certain rites for the dead, to make no fast on Yom Kippur—would be to flaunt the ancestral system of things, to defy the universe, and this is why proposed changes in religious practice are often met with such horror. The sheer endurance of traditional ways of doing things gives tradition itself the weight of sanctity.

Applications of the Sociological Frame

The sociological perspective creates a circle within which all
religious phenomena can be viewed and interpreted. We have
seen how even the concept of sacredness is understood within that
frame. We will now examine further how the two major aspects of
religion, representations or beliefs, and ritual observance, are
both explainable in terms of social function.

Mythologies and Gods. Every tribe has its own version of history
and origins. But these amount to the history and origins *of its own
world.* Moses is not the key figure in Chinese histories. Jesus is not
the key figure in Hindu histories. Muhammed is not the key figure
in Buddhist histories. The New Testament does not begin with a
genealogy of the god Krishna. Japanese Shinto mythologies do not
recite the origin of Babylonian kingship. Planting societies are not
interested in the first buffalo—and hunting societies are not interested in the first yam. Mythology is often genealogy, having to do
with lineages, the origin of culture-specific institutions, and the
time of "our" ancestors.

Mythologies take us back to the great events that founded *our*
society—the first use of corn, the first canoe building, the introduction of the sacred pipe or the sacred commandments, the
teachings of the great sages. Creation myths show how *our* world
came about, our Japanese Islands, our Zuni Mountains, our Sabbath Day, our Holy Land. Sociologically interpreted, the past is
always represented in a way that justifies the present institutions of
society. The world that the supernaturals created reflects the
world of the people whose myth they inhabit. Among the Australian aboriginals, each tribe has a history that recounts the particular things its ancestors did as they traveled throughout the
landscape—a territory that corresponds both to the exact contemporary area of the group *and* to the dreamtime of the mythic
past.

In this context superhuman beings are explainable in sociological terms. Modern people are used to thinking of God as a
supreme principle of some kind, but in traditional religion gods
received their imagery from social categories. They are ancestors,
patriarchs, founders, and patrons of specific communities. They
are rulers and monarchs, masters and matrons of groves, moun-

tains, and animals. They are fathers, mothers, sons, and daughters. People relate to them through forms of social interaction—such as giving and receiving, offering and petitioning, returning gratitude and showing humility.

Gods in this view take their nature and domains from the culture. Whatever life is based on, there is where divinity is projected. Wherever a social world is situated and faces the limits of its own power, there the gods operate. Hence there are gods of one's forest or field, one's family hearth or civic cult. The early depiction of deity in the Bible was as the protector of the destiny of seminomadic herding tribes, as one who would defeat enemies and bring his people to a promised land. Deities take on the value orientation of the society, like monarchical authority,[4] martial power, ritual propriety, ancestry and kinship, even rationality and justice. Correspondingly, behavior toward superhuman beings is an exact expression of the social relationships valued by the culture or subculture; so that gods may be approached through ceremonial decorum, bargaining and cajoling, moral earnestness, wild or ecstatic possession states, wise and reasoned reflection, or love and friendship.

Ritual as a Social Expression. In the sociological view, rites and festivals are not just passed off as prescientific, mistaken efforts to magically control the world, but are seen as exact social languages that encode and express cultural values.

Ritual is first of all a display which is given intensified value by the very fact that it is collectively conducted, witnessed, and experienced. This focused, assembled viewing impresses the reality and validity of the rite and its content upon participants. Political as well as religious rallies show the force of this principle, as do the group silence of a Quaker meeting house and the huddle of a team before a game. To the Durkheimians, part of the meaningfulness of a rite was the way its collective nature created a state of consciousness that transcended the bounds of individual, private experience. The time of assembly is intensified time, the opposite of ordinary, dispersed, working time. The time of ritual makes religious faith seem plausible and real in a way that unconcentrated, nonritual time does not.

For Durkheim the most important function of ritual time was to renew the foundations of society itself, to regenerate the "life" of its beliefs. He observed that each aboriginal tribe had its own annual ceremonies in honor of its totemic species. To participants these ceremonies were ostensibly to increase the fertility of the species (with whom the group believed itself kin) so that more souls for the tribe could be generated. But to the sociologist Durkheim, the real function of the rite was to recreate the identity of the group, an identity that could be expressed only through its objectivization in concrete religious symbols and actions. Again opposing the rationalist view that rituals corresponded to nothing real, he maintained that the rite did indeed have a real function because it actually did renew the tribe's sense of itself and commit- ment to its symbols. Because the participants were renewed, the tribe was renewed. As Durkheim put it, the individual is "dipped again in the source from which its life comes" and consequently is reenergized.[5] Without believing members, society would evapo- rate; without worshipers, the gods would vanish. "Society," Durk- heim wrote, "is able to revivify the sentiment it has of itself only by assembling."[6]

All religions and societies have periodic renewal rites which recall the important values of the group and which renew the liveliness of those values. But whatever the content of different rites, the very act of participating in the rites is an act of renewing one's citizenship in the group. Going to church is an obvious though not trivial example.

A rite or festival allows a group to experience itself in an ideal form. Every society has major occasions where the community shows off its best nature and consolidates its group bonds. This may be done through observances like elaborate feasts, gift ex- changes, visits to relatives or ancestral sites, shared religious dramatizations, public displays, or dressing up in special ways. Festival times showcase to the group the key values of the commu- nity, such as goodwill at Christmastime, the spirit of reconcilia- tion at Yom Kippur, or even toughness and male beauty at Masai warrior initiations.

Ritual can also provide a space in which individuals transcend fixed social roles and experience a sense of equality. Festivals and services may have this effect, as do activities like pilgrimages. The term *liminality* has been used to describe those situations, times, and places where individuals come together in an egalitarian way, free from ascribed status.[7] Here, apart from social hierarchy, a new fellowship is achieved, a new image of sociality is realized. Where people assemble in "the Spirit," society has permitted a new version of itself, transcending racial, political, economic, or gender distinctions. Millions of Muslims on pilgrimage at Mecca experience this unity.

Ritual allows a group and its individuals to act out and experience roles that compensate or complement routine social status, not only in the sense of idealized behaviors but in the sense of moments of license and antistructural activities. In the rite, as it were, one can put on all one's feathers but also take them all off. The varying points of the calendar year give every society a chance to express different aspects of itself serially—now sober, clean, and contrite; now carnivalesque and buoyant; now joyous; now solemn. In such ways, society constructs rites and festivals to give social life its fullest scope of expression.

Great annual festivals are major displays of social values. For groups whose way of life is based on rivalry with neighboring tribes, the festivals often oscillate between rites of victory and of mourning. In collectivity-oriented East Asian society the New Year Festival focuses on the family and ancestry. Southeast Asian cultures based on the polarity of monastics and laity have strategic, annual festivals reenacting the ideal relationship of the two. Traditional monarchical societies made a yearly production about regenerating the prestige of the institution of kingship. Socialist societies have festivals celebrating their proletarian ideals about the value of work; meditation societies on their special occasions intensify their meditation; secret, exclusive sects have secret, exclusive annual rites. Whatever the most important relationships in a society, they will be displayed in the major periodic festivals. Thus the world of a society is continuously recreated. Without rite and ceremony societies fail to communicate and maintain the vigor and sacredness of their own foundations.

Rites of passage[8]—those occasions which celebrate transitions in life—are ways of relating individual changes to the overall domain of the community. Even secular societies have them. Without the group, social status remains undefined. Rites of birth, coming-to-adulthood, marriage, and death place individuals in new, consolidated relations to the group, into a network of membership. New leadership is given prestige and legitimation by public inaugurations. At the same time, what one culture may consider a significant moment of change, others may completely ignore. One's first kill may be ritually celebrated in one culture, while in another what might be singled out is the moment of eligibility to vote.

Finally, religious observances often involve behaviors con-nected with purity.[9] Some groups have highly defined purity rules for maintaining membership, keeping social and religious identity free from compromise—for example, kosher food laws or rules about abstinence from drinking may symbolize the separateness of the members from the surrounding social norms.

Kinds of Society: Kinds of Religion

The important and influential work of the German sociologist Max Weber (1864–1920) opened up the systematic study of how types of religious outlooks correlate with types of social values.[10] In this view, religion absorbs and then mirrors back the ethical and ideological orientation of different social classes. Confucian-ism, for example, represented the ideals of statesmen and bureau-crats; early Buddhism the viewpoint of mendicant monks; and Judaism that of a minority culture. As Christianity evolved, its ideas about what it meant to be Christian reflected the interests of very different kinds of social classes. Christianity could thus be otherworldly, this-worldly, or a combination of both, depending on how its social and economic life was situated. Concepts like salvation, future compensation, sin, or even religious humility are natural to certain social classes and not to others—among Web-er's best known distinctions are those between the religions of the nonprivileged (hence the need for salvation) and the privi-leged (who have no need for a salvation because they are already "sated").

Consider a few representative examples of ways that types of religion reflect types of society.

Religion and Historical Forms of Social Organization. One typology distinguishes broadly different kinds of historical cultures, for example (1) small-scale or tribal, (2) traditional monarchical city-state, and (3) large and highly differentiated.

In the first type, religious life, like economic life, is ordinarily diffused throughout the social system rather than being a distinct, separate institution. Religious symbols and rites reflect direct economic dependency on animal or plant life, and also show the sacredness of ancestors, kinship, and social status generally.

In the second type, represented in ancient city-states and kingdoms, a highly specialized religious organization forms, with a distinct class of priests. Religious specialists comprise a hierarchy parallel to the centralization and prestige of political power in the authority of a king, and the residences of the patron gods parallel the residences of kings. The typical religious acts in this kind of society are worship and service of the gods—again analogous to the relationship of subjects to kings. Sacrifice to the gods, reflecting the subservience of individual ownership to overarching lordship, is also a feature.

A third type of society is the large-scale, religiously noncentralized kind. This type is seen in many modern nation-states, but also throughout history wherever culture is amorphous enough so that subcommunities become the most vital media of religious affiliation and expression. Religious organizations here are subgroups within a larger culture. When the biblical Israelites ceased to be a kingdom, they became such a culture within a culture, a highly defined community held together through its own ideology, rituals, and indices of membership. In some ways this was to become the prototype of Christianity, originally a sect of people banded together with their own vision within the larger Roman empire. The hierarchic and centralized city-state model reappeared, however, when Catholic Christianity assumed some of the structure of Roman imperial government. Most modern secular constitutions comfortably tolerate the proliferation of sectarian religious groups.

Such types show but one spectrum of possible relationships of religion to society. At the one end religion is not an independent entity; in the middle, it is associated with strong, centralized kingdoms and its behavior reflects patterns of hierarchic authority; and at the other end religion becomes a self-contained subsociety within a culture, positing its own system of religious values and membership.

Institutionalization and Innovation. Another sociological distinction acknowledges two opposite tendencies in religion, corresponding to two opposite activities of social formation. The first is the consolidation of institutional self-preservation, and the second is the movement toward innovation and challenge to existing social institutions. Religion can have opposite functions relative to social order, and often these two phases of activity can be found within the same religious tradition.

The institutionalization of religion is the legitimation of bureaucratic and hierarchic categories, which functions to protect religious authority from subversion and to enforce behavioral codes. This is partly because religion is put in a defensive position in relation to the rest of society. The more there is to protect, the more there is to defend. But institutionalization is also a function of size and efficiency. The larger the religion, the more structure and channels of authority will be necessary.

In contrast are religious movements formed out of dissatisfaction with mainstream institutional values and which break off to form new communities typically inspired by charismatic leadership. Sects or new religious movements correspond to the need for new social bonds in cultures where life has been specifically disrupted (such as in the rootlessness caused by the transition from village to urban life) or because of outright intellectual dissent from ruling ideologies or social values. New religions are society's way of creating communities based on similar values. The thousands of sects found around the world have much of their appeal in their ability to provide people with alternative families and roots in the midst of urban chaos and mobility.

Religion versus Society or "the World." Religious movements that oppose themselves to society or even "the world" comprise a large variety of types.

In biblical times there originated a movement in which prophets challenged routine cult observances in the name of a higher piety. The prophets were manifestations of the capacity of religion to critique religion. When in their view the official cult became too self-serving and unreligious, they spoke out against its established corruption. When the emphasis on ritual fastidiousness overshadowed the emphasis on ethics and justice, they railed against the falseness of the socially approved sacred practices. Later, Muhammed and the Protestant reformers continued in this same critical spirit.

Fundamentalism is a worldwide religious phenomenon that is not difficult to interpret sociologically. It typically arises where the pace of modernity threatens to be overwhelming. The solution appears in the form of a return to the absoluteness of scripture and divine laws. Against the chaos of secularization it opposes the rock of supernatural certainty, inerrancy, and authority. Against the ambiguity of secular morality it hurls the unambiguous meanings of religious fundamentals. While non-fundamentalist Westerners are used to thinking of these movements as forms of naive belief, the widespread presence of these movements in modern cultures that face secularity shows the sociologist that doctrinal absoluteness is really a concomitant of a group's social strategy. Muslim, Jewish, Hindu, and Buddhist fundamentalists all believe in different absolutes, but they all have the similar socio-cultural function of creating hedges from the past against the uncontrollable promiscuity of modern behavior and thought.

Salvation-type religions have many variants. Religions of redemption appeal to social classes that are marginalized or oppressed by ruling social power systems and cultural values; or to intellectual upper classes for whom higher meanings supersede the banal values of mainstream society. In either case what is sought is a strong alternative, another world in which one's true identity may be found. This world is typically projected onto another space, like heaven, a coming period of divine rule, or another spiritual status, like nirvana or "God within."

Both Christianity and Buddhism began as religions of liberation from the powers of "this world." The first sought transition to a coming "kingdom of God"—conceived in either heavenly or earthly terms—thus continuing Jewish concepts of future vindication and messianic fulfillment, and establishing a prototype for all biblically inspired, adventist-type sects that have continued to serve the needs of socially unintegrated or disenfranchised populations. The wickedness of present society, in which life is subjected to indignity, is in these groups juxtaposed with the blessedness and justification of a future society, in which dignity will be bestowed. The poor and socially downtrodden will paradoxically be receivers of the wealth of God's new order. "Blessed are those who are persecuted for righteousness' sake," says the New Testament, "for theirs is the kingdom of heaven" (Matt. 5:10). Christianity in particular has a strong redemptive element at its core, more so than either Judaism or Islam. "My kingship," Jesus announces, "is not of this world" (John 18:36).

In the case of Buddhism, dissatisfaction with the world took an ideological rather than a political form. The problem of society was not the corruptness of governments but the inadequacy of ordinary social values and identities. Here the problem of society became a problem of meaning, and the solution was the Buddha's teaching, which showed the path to recreating one's existence through the radical, meditative way of the renunciate. This spiritual discipline was in effect a way of reversing one's socialization and its wheel of unrealizable desires, its chain of birth-sex-rebirth, of endless desire-laden karma. Early Buddhism created an order of monks who vowed to give up attachments to all the entrapments of ordinary social existence in order to seek a state of peace and enlightenment. The Buddhist teachings speak of "breaking the ridgepole" of the house of ignorance, and of seeking a life of freedom and purity through an alternative, monastic community. All possessions were to be abandoned, except for a yellow robe, razor, and begging bowl, symbols of the possessionless state itself. One of the attractions of early Buddhism was its offering of freedom from family and caste roles.

A later, popular form of Buddhism—to this day the largest denomination of Japanese Buddhism—developed an elaborate conception of a "Pure Land" to which "the lowest of the low, the worst of sinners" could be delivered upon practicing faith in the power of Amida Buddha. Buddhism hitherto had been largely a monastic enterprise, but now there arose a need for a version for laypersons, whose position in the world was more precarious.

Thus there are religious worldviews in which the social world itself is part of the problem which requires religious solution. Society in its ordinary state ceases to be a home base and becomes a "profane" order to be transcended, a place of fallenness, sin, or ignorance, a place from which we need to be saved. "The sacred" here plays a different, more dynamic role than in the Durkheimian idea of totemic solidarity, being more a matter of holy disengagement and holy dissent.

One of the most obvious forms of redemptive religion is the sect which forms as a direct response to social oppression.[11] Ideas of salvation here are compensatory beliefs that make life livable and justifiable in circumstances which are neither. Thus the idea of a messianic kingdom grew in attraction to Jews during the time of great political persecution. Early Christianity drew many recruits from slaves. Belief in redemptive religion is a typical strategy of peoples oppressed by colonialism. The Ghost Dance movement in the late nineteenth century drew American Plains Indians to a belief in the coming of a new era that would restore Indian culture and dissolve oppressive white rule. The Black Muslim sect developed an analogous ideology which highlighted the superiority of blacks and the wickedness of whites. Rastafarians in a Jamaica ruled by whites developed a passionate mythology of a future return to Africa under the leadership of an African messiah.

Religions construct new identities in other ways than through countermythologies. An example is the possession cult. Social systems that encourage trance and possession by gods and spirits thereby permit huge ranges of nonordinary behavior. From a sociological perspective, these allow direct empowerment and status enhancement to the status-deprived. To the socially repressed they may also offer unrepressed ecstasy, wild physical display, or other actions that would otherwise be completely unacceptable. Possession phenomena become not only legitimizations of multiple roles and personalities, but sheer social theater. One anthropologist describes an East African society which has a system of women's possession rites—which the reporter calls "strategies for protest"—that allows wives under the influence of spirits to verbally attack their husbands with no repercussions whatsoever.[12] Spirit trance becomes social drama. In such ways social explanation can appear to be inclusive and sufficient.[13]

What of the individual hermit who has forsaken all groups? The sociological interpretation is that eremitism occurs in societies which allow for that kind of withdrawal and give a certain value to it. The case of India illustrates this well. Within its society all stations of life are given legitimacy. The final stage, that of the renunciate (the *sannyasin*), allows individuals to abandon all their previous social identity, including their name, and enter a life of pure contemplation. There are millions of *sannyasins* in India, and yet their presence cannot be said to contradict the social basis of religion. It is society that has created them, that has produced the concept of its own internal and graduated forms of renunciation. This is why monasteries and hermitages are social institutions, as is modern individualism.

In these ways the sociological frame of interpretation appears capacious enough to account for whole ranges of religious groups, including otherworldly types. It is the natural activity of society not only to create internal bonds but to differentiate into subsocieties and even invent new interpretations of the world.

Religious Systems as Social Syntheses. We have seen that in spite of the "world religions" textbook image that there is a finite handful of religions in the world whose beliefs can concisely be summarized, the sociocultural approach acknowledges as many actual religious systems as there are actual kinds of societies and subsocieties in history. Here official doctrine reveals less about the nature of religion than do the ways in which religious ideas are used, practiced, or integrated within a given cultural context. The life of religion is in its social reality. The emergence, for example, of hundreds of versions of Buddhism, Christianity, and Islam corresponded to the play of as many different strategies and syncretisms of social empowerment.

New religious movements often have this combinatory appeal, recreating symbols and observances to mirror exactly their cultural needs. While, numerically speaking, Christianity is the largest religion in the world, in actuality it takes myriads of social and hence religious forms. Thus in modern Brazil, syncretistic, spiritist religions like Umbanda have become pervasive. Umbanda is an urban religion in which Catholic saints coalesce with African spirits; the spirits of old slaves and Brazilian Indians are also important entities in its pantheon. In effect it incorporates the realities of its own multi-ethnic social scene—African, Indian, and European—into a kind of unified divine consortium of spirit powers. It creates a religious synthesis that fits the social horizon.

The example repeats itself worldwide, where the imported religion finds itself expressed through regional practices, empowerments, associations, and interpretations. For instance, one product of contemporary American culture is the "megachurch" that accommodates the needs, styles, and language of an electronic, pragmatic, and even entertainment-oriented society. Trans-denominational superbuildings seat thousands in theater-type formats and are usually connected with television ministries. Attached to the churches are dozens of highly organized activity and service groups, addressing issues like substance abuse, sexuality and marriage counseling, financial planning, AIDS and poverty, and problems of the blind and deaf. Youth activities include sports teams, Christian rock music, and discussions of teen concerns like peer pressure and family breakups. The administrative centers of the churches are physically indistinguishable from urban business buildings. The result is the creation of a world that perfectly fuses religion with aspects and styles of a contemporary society. Japanese new religions also show many parallel examples of such blendings and streamlined modern applications.

Reflections on the Social Frame

The strengths of the sociological frame are the huge amount of information it discovers about the contextual nature of religious life, and the strong, varied relationships it uncovers between religious and sociocultural identity. Its angle of vision shows aspects of religiousness that are not understood in strictly doctrinal or even rationalist approaches. The sociocultural view shows that religion can be seen as a significant form of cultural behavior rather than as something either revealed from on high that is "true," or something made up by the prescientific mind that is "false." It is a lens that draws close attention to religion's tremendously diverse social matrices and gives a clear account of why religion takes such different forms.

To analyze the limits of this explanatory frame is to return again to issues about the perspectival nature of interpretation. What, for example, does the social frame *not* see? What are the limits of its view? What are its assumptions?

As noted in chapter 2, to explain religion by the concept of society or culture may give the impression that something formerly considered mysterious and unknown is finally being grounded in something unmysterious and known. On the surface, this seems to be the case, but ultimately the nature of an entity like "society" is not at all clear and fixed. Calling human life "society" draws attention to certain aspects of culture, but does not close off the larger issue of what human life "is." To say that everything can be explained in terms of *society* or *culture* may appear to explain the question of human existence, but these terms also become easy spaces for the projection of the interpreter's own representations of existence. If we say that religion is explained by culture, the question remains, "What is culture?" In effect the answer is, "Whatever the sociologist or anthropologist—either implicitly or explicitly—thinks it is." Religion comes from the depths of our own being, says Durkheim—it is us. But "us" according to whom? According to which of us? Whose culture is our model, and which philosophy of culture?

Society and *culture* on the surface may seem to describe observable traditions of behavior, language, and institutions, and may not seem to have further philosophical or ontological status. But they implicitly come to have philosophical status if they are used to affirm that religion is *only* social behavior.

Social scientists themselves do not have a uniform model of society or culture. The sociocultural frame is shifting and selective, not monolithic, and it changes with social history. Insofar as the interpreter's own culture goes through shifts in ideas about religion, theory itself is always in historical motion and a phenomenon to be studied in its own right.[14] We have seen a sequence of very different anthropological perceptions of religion, from haughty nineteenth-century interests in "savage" mentalities, to highly sophisticated twentieth-century interests in cultures as complex systems of symbolic classification. Western sociologists often focus on topics like secularization or church-state conflicts. Each generation or interpreter uses theories shaped to particular questions and horizons.

While the social frame is a revealing and useful one, it does not necessarily disallow other levels of explanation. It is conceivable that a theologian could accept the idea that religion is socially contextual while still maintaining that humans connect with a real, supernatural being *through* the particularities of social setting. Behavior can also be explained in terms of physiology, but few would want to say that physical and sociological explanations are mutually exclusive. It is one thing to show that religion correlates with social context, but it is another to show that the social context is the sole cause of religion.

The very idea that society creates religion is not a falsifiable proposition, but an interpretive frame that draws attention to certain kinds of relationships which become its data. Moreover, if religion is really created by society, then, as Durkheim stressed, it *is* society; and to say "society creates society" is an obvious but rather empty and circular claim. There does not yet seem to be any way to conduct an empirical test that would determine whether human life is ultimately "social" or not—just as there is no experiment that can be done to determine the nature of human existence.

Culture is filled with radically different modes of experience, like microphysics, music, and visual arts. While all of these activities can be objects of sociological analysis, their nature is not wholly encapsulated or described in that analysis. They have their own points of view, their own world that they "see" and create within society. The investigation of what biological, musical, and aesthetic worlds look like as data on their own terms gave rise to the separate fields—one might say the separate lenses—of biology, musicology, and art history. We shall see in chapter 5 how the decision to look at religious subject matter as a special type of experience led to the creation of the modern field of comparative religion. In short, society includes more than "social" experience.

Yet even social expressions are complex and enigmatic blends of meanings, imageries, and values which require interpretive work similar to that given a piece of literature. The anthropologist Clifford Geertz, known for his style of reading social behaviors as complex, nuanced texts thus writes, "Believing, with Max Weber, that man is an animal suspended in webs of significance he himself has spun, I take culture to be those webs, and the analysis of it to be therefore not an experimental science in search of law but an interpretive one in search of meaning."[15]

If social science thinks in terms of general laws and principles, then the unique and creative aspects of culture tend to get left out of sociological analyses. And yet all culture, history, and experience has a once-only character, a one-time combination of horizons that is difficult to see with lenses that only scan in terms of generalities.

We have seen that even within the sociological frame religions have a certain creative force. The same could be said of science and art, and even of individual personalities. If we are created by society, we also create it. For example, we can abandon our society and take up another one. We can become aware of many of our socially constructed biases and attempt to overcome them. The idea that "we *are* society" then takes on an open-ended aspect. The produced (religion) is also the producer. The projections (the beliefs, gods, ideas, ideals, and moral visions) are also agencies with effective lives of their own. Thus religion itself can be a way of interpreting society. If religion can transcend society in practice, it can also do so in theory.

Although social theory sees the individual psyche as part of social life, in many important ways each individual is a unique psychological agency in his or her own right, and as such is clearly an organizing source of culture. Individual creativity, whether explained in terms of an unconscious or in terms of personality, has generated much of what we consider to be great or powerful in culture.

Thus the factors of uniqueness, creativity, and autonomy challenge the totalizing, generalizing nature of social analysis.

Ironically, on purely sociological grounds we could say that within our culture there are needs for many types and levels of self-interpretation other than social interpretation. These levels correspond to the many kinds of questions raised within society and to the variety of symbol systems within society. The language of sociology then becomes just one discourse, one linguistic act and frame among several, each of which correlates with different levels of seeing, audiences, social positionings, and intellectual needs. After all, interpretations—of any kind—are themselves cultural acts that belong with specific cultural contexts. In the labs, science is spoken; in the churches, religion is spoken.

For example, what if we look at religion not sociologically but psychologically? A different range of data comes into view, the gods take on a different hue and shape, and religion becomes a different phenomenon altogether.

4

As the Psyche, So the Gods

Just as the sociology of religion went well beyond Marx, so the psychology of religion went well beyond Freud. An outstanding example of a broad, psychological interpretation of religion is that of Carl Gustav Jung (1875–1961) and his circle of influence.[1] Jung attributed to the psyche a creative power comparable to that which Durkheim attributed to society. Where social anthropology looked outward to the role of culture, the "depth psychology" of Jung looked inward to the role of the unconscious, and in their readings of religious symbols the Jungians focused on areas of experience untouched by a sociological level of analysis.

In this chapter the Jungian approach to religion is the interpretive lens.

The Concept of the Unconscious: From Freud to Jung

At the turn of the century the Swiss Jung and the Viennese Freud were colleagues in the formation of the new science of psychoanalysis, and Freud, nineteen years older, saw Jung as his intellectual heir during this time. Both were committed to advancing a new framework for explaining human behavior, one that pictured humans in terms of the relation between a conscious but fragile ego and the unconscious.

The unconscious includes all those things about oneself that for one reason or another one is incapable of making conscious. Humans in this theory are not just reasoning machines or "minds" composed of the faculties of reason, volition, and feeling, but

48

psychological beings whose consciousness develops in the course of a lifetime. Depending on how they relate to the contents of the unconscious, egos can be defensive and neurotic, creating techniques for avoiding unacceptable parts of the self, or they can be instruments of increased self-awareness and change.

In the years following 1912 Jung broke with Freud on the grounds that his famous friend's model was too narrowly conceived, and that a broader notion of the psyche had to be constructed.[2] In Jung's view the Freudian unconscious was limited to a place where the ego puts all its repressed personal past—something like a basement where traumas, unacceptable desires, and unresolved psychological knots of various kinds are stored but active. Although these contents are suppressed, their very unconscious status rules our lives until they are brought forth by the light of psychoanalysis.

In contrast to this "basement" image, Jung posited a broader schema, one that saw the unconscious not just as a garbage bin but more like a mansion with many types of rooms. In Jung's view the unconscious was as deep and many-leveled as the world itself, reflecting the creative as well as the pathological functions of life. If Freud was oriented to comprehending and untying the ego's past, Jung was primarily interested in the ego's transformations and future development. As a rationalist, Freud saw the unconscious as subrational and thought that the ego needed to strengthen its own rationality to gain maturity. Jung, in contrast, thought that one-sided rationality was not the end point of the ego's evolution, and that a "wholeness" of one's selfhood was also an important goal.

Here is where religion comes in. While for Freud religious symbols were ironic, disguised fragments of one's unresolved childhood, for Jung they might also function as positive mediators between the ego and a deeper part of the self, i.e., as active agencies of psychological change and recentering. If the gods represent projections of dependency relationships, they also represent projections of ego-transcendence and an emerging, larger self-consciousness.

Psyche as Matrix

Jung's key term for the totality of conscious and unconscious life is the *psyche*. For Jung the psyche is not just individual, but also has a collective dimension. It does not begin anew with each individual; rather, individuals inherit its structures just as they do the structures of their bodies. In this sense the psyche is not something contained within individuals, but individuals are participants in it. The psyche is for Jung what society is for Durkheim: the matrix of all experience. We cannot see the world except through it. It is the great, silent medium we take for granted. We do not know its limits. We do not control it. "If we want to understand the psyche," Jung said, "we have to include the whole world."[3]

Jung thought of his work as descriptive rather than metaphysical. He did not claim to know what was outside, underneath, or behind the collective psyche, nor did he think that religious thinkers had privileged information about an ultimate reality beyond it. Every position about truth, reality, the meaning of life, the nature and existence of gods—in short, every worldview—was itself inevitably a position reflecting a certain psychological orientation. According to Jung, we can observe the psyche's workings but we cannot assume a position over and beyond them.

Jung viewed the language of religion as part of the natural language of the psyche: religious thought does not tell us what the universe is, but reveals the way the psyche symbolizes itself. In Jung's exchanges with biblical theologians who accused him of reducing God to the unconscious, he challenged them to produce an image of God that was *not* part of the matrix of psychic experience but which stood outside it in some objective sense.

A major part of Jung's idea of psyche is that the unconscious has some autonomy or creativity of its own. It is an instrument of change and development; a responsive, even compensatory counterpoint to the life of the ego. Dreams are one of its primary activities, obviously functioning independently of the conscious will and even at times contradicting conscious attitudes and emotions. For Jung the unconscious is the source of intuitions and inspirations as well as the source of slips of the tongue and embarrassments. It works in conjunction with the lives of artists and religious people as well as the lives of schizophrenics and hypochondriacs.

Thus to theologians who insisted that God is what is outside us, Jung agreed that, yes, a god is *experienced* as "other" than the ego and as outside ourselves—so is the devil—because the ego experiences itself as a recipient of powers that do not seem to be its own. These powers can be inspiring or depressing. Gods and demons are the ego's experience of aspects of the unconscious itself. To Jung religiousness is the "careful consideration and observation" of "other" powers that impinge upon our life, and yet are part of our life, and which we neglect at our own risk.[4]

This view of the unconscious as a region which actively influences the life of the ego gave Jung a model for interpreting religious experience. Gods here become symbols of the unconscious; religious experiences like conversion or the felt "grace of God" translate into ways in which the ego undergoes transformations in relation to its own psychic ground or by which a wider self is re-created.

Archetypes of the Unconscious

Just as common types of social organization like the family, tribe, or secret society may be found in different cultures, so typical kinds of ego orientations are found throughout human culture. The psyche, like society and like the body, operates in patterned ways. The Jungian "archetypes" are the typical, impelling patterns or situations in which the human ego finds itself in relation to the unconscious. They are the psychological versions of the instincts. Whereas for Freud the Oedipus myth, with its parental attraction-aggression pattern, is the singular archetype of ego development, Jungian psychology expands the notion of patterns to recognize a plurality of archetypes representing several stages of ego development. As we shall see, the central goal of the mature psyche for Jung is what he called the realization of the archetype of "the self."

Stages of Ego Development/Stages of Mythology.[5] Like social history, ego development unfolds in such a way that one stage presupposes a preceding one as its condition. Social history does not begin with kingdoms or with monasteries, but with clans and tribes. Likewise psychological history, the development of consciousness in an individual, has certain stadial moments. Post-Freudian psychologists schematize these differently, but usually identify the key stages of (1) dependency, (2) autonomy, and (3) integration. For Jungians each of these corresponds to levels of religious experience and types of mythological images.

1. The first stage is that of the containment of the unformed ego by its original nourishing matrix. This is a state of complete dependency on the mother or environment. The ego has at first no separate identity, but gradually acquires some awareness of its difference from the mother while still being under her aegis. This stage corresponds to the transition from infancy to childhood.

To some extent Freudians and Jungians would agree about the way this first ego-context translates into mythological images. We have already seen examples of this stage in the projected symbolisms of a blissful, trouble-free state, such as a primal Garden of Eden, a Golden Age, or an all-supplying mother goddess.

Corresponding with the emergence of ego consciousness and the subsequent appearance of ambivalent relationships embodying emotions like trust and fear, are mythologies of nurturing and devouring, protection and punishment. For at this point the ego, now more conscious but highly uncertain, is still at the mercy of the containing authority, i.e., parents-gods. At this stage the parents-gods show fluctuating qualities corresponding to the oscillating relationship of the ego to the beneficent and threatening features of authority. The inconstancy of the character of gods reflects the inconstancy of this ego-authority relationship.

2. The second general psychological stage is that of the ego's increasing autonomy, the process of its differentiation from an original dominating or containing force. This stage correlates with adolescence and the process of becoming an adult. Separation from external authority has the aspects both of freeing oneself from a subordinate position and of recentering or internalizing authority in oneself. Both of these developments are expressed in rites of initiation, in which one undergoes the ordeal of separation from childhood ego-dependencies, but also the internalization of adult responsibilities. It has been noted that there is a special tendency for males to need to differentiate themselves from their mothers through acts of "killing" the old relationship (or the old ego) in various ways, such as clarifying male-female difference by identification with the father and rejection of the mother. Monasticism, with its rejection of worldly ties and its stress on self-dedication, reflects a later and more committed aspect of this stage. So does membership in special or secret societies, which enhances the ego's sense of differentiation from the larger group while at the same time emphasizing its own sense of special identity. The disobedience and expulsion scene in the Garden of

Eden story gives mythic imagery to this need for separation from the womb of origin.

Mythologies of violence and monster-slaying reflect part of this stage also. Psychologically, the confrontation and defeat of demons or dragons objectivizes and corresponds to the ego's act of overcoming the powers that oppress it. The dragon, as in the fairy tales, holds the treasure in its territory but does not have use for it itself. It is therefore a symbol of both tyranny and fear, awaiting the courage of the ego to challenge its false and paralyzing authority in order to redeem the kept treasure. The process of facing and overcoming fear parallels the ordeals of the maturing ego—mythologically expressed in innumerable motifs about "the hero."

To Jungians, hero myths symbolize ways in which ego formation takes place through struggle, suffering, and sacrifice.[6] Typically, a form of mortification is required—descending into some kind of hell, being swallowed by a monster, or being lost. These "deaths" symbolize detachment from the hero's own past ego, and readiness for "rebirth" to a new self. The treasure to be won by effort represents the new part of the psyche, the liberation of which makes further development possible.

3. Once the ego has become independent, it sooner or later has to face its own weaknesses and undeveloped sides, its own lack of wholeness. Consciousness and resolution of the self-generated sources of one's own internal conflictual nature now become an inner task. This self-integration is the challenge of adulthood or "the second half of life," constituting a psychological journey that has often and traditionally been conceived in religious vocabularies. Self-monitoring, self-accountability and responsibility, "knowing oneself," indeed, wisdom—these are the stages of self-development for which religions and spiritual philosophies have historically supplied the conceptual, mythological frameworks. Symbols and paths of inner wholeness and peace, "mystical marriage," and the harmony of opposites (e.g., yin and yang) correspond to this time of psychological synthesis.

It is the characteristic Jungian contribution to have created a systematic, translative connection between types of religious paths and types of psychological processes. Here the psychology of religious development can be understood as an intelligible form of behavior, apart from the truth-claims of the specific religious ideologies in which the life of the ego has so traditionally and thoroughly been encased.

In all of these processes the psyche is conspiratorial, reflecting back an environment correlative with the status and activity of the ego. The unconscious is both the dragon and the lover, the projection screen of fear and the collaborative center of the soul's development. It is in this latter regard that Jung formulated the central concept of an archetype of "the self."

The Self Archetype. In the years following his separation with Freud, Jung experienced a crisis of his own, a personal re-centering accompanied by extraordinary, unsolicited imagistic material from his own unconscious. He resigned his academic post and submitted to the changes he was undergoing and which he felt he could not entirely resist. What emerged was his appreciation of the transformative nature of the unconscious, a view that was to become a feature of his post-Freudian psychology. In particular, he had come upon an understanding that a certain, strong archetype was at work in his experiences, one that he termed "the self."

Here was the emergence of the concept that the ego not only connects backward to past factors like sexuality, but also forward to its own transformations in new forms of self-identity, value orientation, and wholeness. "The self" concept provided a framework for explaining the extraordinary role religious and mythic symbols play in human experience. "Strictly speaking, the God-image does not coincide with the unconscious as such, but with a special content of it, namely the archetype of the self. It is this archetype from which we can no longer distinguish the God-image empirically."[7] In other words, it is part of the natural activity of the psyche to produce "god-images." This production is a function of the emergence of consciousness and consequent reforming of the ego in terms of a larger self.

Just as the ego is the center of one's conscious personality, the self in Jung's view is the organizational totality of one's conscious and unconscious life. The power of religious images of deity is therefore not just to represent ego-dependency (as Freud might say), but also to activate the self, which in some ways helps to overcome the neuroses and weaknesses of the ego. This interpretive model allowed Jungian psychology to translate religious language about the relationship of humanity and divinity into the dynamics of the ego-self relation.

For Jungians the self can be experienced by the ego as something outer or inner. Most egos are too fragile and uncertain to relate to the self in any other way than through projections onto others. Power here does not seem to lie within. The self then is typically "other," or idealized, as in the form of a god, savior, or spiritual teacher, but can also be represented in objects like spatial designs, circles or mandalas, temples, or anything that has the imagery of a defined center, autonomous life, enduring power, secret knowledge, and so on. Yet several strands of religious thought also appeal to an inner source. Here is the language about a God or Buddha within, an eternal soul, an inner spark of divinity or inner ally, a higher self within everyone, or even what the Greeks called one's "daimon."

The self-ego relation will therefore vary. The different ways that the self is conceived will correspond to different types of egos, so that gods appear as tyrants and lovers, mothers and fathers, heroes and friends, powers and presences, transcendent and immanent, outsiders and insiders.

Interpreting the History of Religion

With the identification of an interpretive frame in which the history of religion becomes the history of symbols of the ego-self relationship, we can now illustrate more fully how the model applies to the interpretation of religious data.

Goddesses and Kings. Jungians typically identify an age of the goddess as preceding the rise of male-oriented god-king mythologies with their emphasis on hierarchy and power.[8] This conforms to the view that "the Great Mother" is the symbol for the unconscious itself prior to the rise of ego development. In the realm of the goddess, the unconscious psyche is in a state of nature, containing equally and cyclically the opposite forces of fertility and decay, nurture and destruction. As nature is no respecter of individual egos, neither is the great goddess. Goddesses rule the coming and going of plant and animal life, the rhythms of the earth. Iconographically the goddess appears to be the original ruler of the tree of life and its mythic garden—long before the writers of the Hebrew Garden of Eden story retold the myth and made Eve a human seductress and secondary character to Adam.

A psychology of rule replacing a psychology of nature was expressed in the emergence of strong political kingdoms, for example in the Near East. As the goddess mythologies drew on agricultural imagery, the male mythologies of divine kingship drew on the imagery of political power, a phenomenon reflected in the outlook of the Hebrew Bible. The goddesses are banished from its pages, as the impulse toward the territorial nature of a highly defined moral and political order assumed control over against the threatening, unpredictable energies of the earth with its multitude of nonrational powers. Psychologically, culture creates a bulwark of male-dominated authority that functions to solidify the autonomy of ego-consciousness against the ambiguous forces of Mother Nature. Interpreted through the eyes of male consciousness, goddesses then tended to be divided into positive and negative types, embodiments either of inspiring purity and goodness or of menacing fury and violence.

The rise of Buddhism and Christianity as mythologies of liberation and world-renunciation exemplified to Jungians the capacity of the psyche to disengage from the "wheel of the world" (i.e., the great mother, the container of the ego, nature) by postulating a higher level of self-identity (nirvana, kingdom of heaven, the self archetype). According to Jung, as we shall see, the price of this new identity was typically an inner war between the earthy, human side of the self and its "higher" spiritual side, a conflict that gave rise to new problems but also to new integrative solutions.

Biblical Religion. Jung thought that it was particularly important for Westerners to understand the psychological foundation of biblical god-images.[9] The older strata of the Bible pictured a god (Yahweh) that appeared to be a projection of an unformed, "amoral" stage of ego development: Yahweh's behavior is "lacking in self-reflection," inflated with self-power, "unconscious" of the needs of others, and ruled by the emotions of anger and vengeance.[10] The god of the book of Job projects his own lack of insight onto the innocent and suffering human being. God's sarcastic, defensive, and belligerent thunderings at Job, after all that Job has gone through, are avoidance mechanisms covering his own guilt at causing this human being to be tortured in the first place, and also miss the point of Job's sensitive, honest questions about why he has had to suffer. In his tremendous speech from the whirlwind, Yahweh repeatedly feels the need to stress his own "righteousness"—significantly, since it is the quality he lacks. His description of the sea and earth monsters he has created (Le-

viathan and Behemoth), with their impenetrable coats of mail
and their hearts as "hard as stone" is a self-description. His railings
are really self-incriminations veiled as accusations of Job; e.g.,
"Who is this that darkens counsel by words without knowledge?"
and "Shall a faultfinder contend with the Almighty?"

For Jung, succeeding phases of Yahweh's image show a certain
development of consciousness. The god-image, like the adult ego,
transforms through experience. Thus the doctrine of the compas-
sionate incarnation of God in human flesh suggests a certain
humanization of awareness. In his incarnation in a human body,
Yahweh drinks the cup of human suffering. When Jesus cries out
on the cross, "My God, my God, why hast thou forsaken me?"
Yahweh has finally experienced what Job did. He begins to experience humanity.

Horrifically described in the last book of the Bible, the book
of Revelation, is a state of conflict described as the contest between "the sons of light" and "the sons of darkness." A war in the
psyche has emerged, now not between the earth goddesses and the
authority of cultural order, but a moral war within. It is expressed
outwardly as a showdown between the elect and the wicked, but is
psychologically the dualism of the Christian and the recalcitrant,
non- or anti-Christian halves of the self. It becomes a mythological conflict between the legions of God and the legions of Satan,
which perpetuates itself well into modern times.

To Jung the ego has become divided against itself. The ten-
sion occurs because one side makes a tremendous claim which
identifies goodness with a particular institutional symbol and
commitment, a claim that is as inwardly and unconsciously fragile
as it is outwardly absolute. The inward doubt cannot be faced
directly and inwardly, and so is experienced as an opposition to
outer "sons of darkness" and resisted at that level. The factor
which makes us vulnerable within, such as doubt, is the factor
that we are so quick to notice and criticize in others.

All of this dualistic religious mythology is read in Jungian
terms as a dreamlike projection of an egoic state that is still
capable only of externalizing its fears. The Jungian term for this is
shadow projection. The *shadow* is the unseen part of the ego—
unseen because it is not comfortable for one reason or another to
accept it. It is the weakness that the ego tries to cover. But
unusual, adamant rage at certain traits in others usually indicates
that it is precisely that element in others that represents or

prompts the ego's *own* self-doubt and vulnerability. Hence the outbursts and accusations about demons, especially in places and times where holiness or purity are strongly asserted. In psychoanalysis the first, essential step in clarifying any subsequent self-understanding is to get people to face up to their own shadows.

This is why the Christian God and the Christian Devil inevitably became parts of a single worldview. Wherever there is a strong, one-sided affirmation, the opposite of it tends to appear. Just as gods are projections of our empowerments, so enemies and demons are projections of our fears.

In making light and dark completely irreconcilable, separate entities, humans abandon the incentive to identify the origin of evil within themselves. In the belief that God is defined as one side of a dualism of light and darkness—"God is light and in him is no darkness at all," reads the scripture (1 John 1:15)—the psyche insulates itself from introspection and self-accountability. Evil comes from out there, not in here. The "New Jerusalem" to come is only for the elect, while Satan remains loose and at large.

This duality gave Jung cause for concern. He became especially interested in forms of spirituality—he found it in most religious traditions—which attempted to acknowledge a "whole" self that superseded mythic splittings of male and female, spiritual ("higher") and earthy ("lower") elements, and inner and outer reality. In some ways, the differentiation of opposites itself created the basis and opportunity for their resolution. For example, in spite of the official doctrines of deity in male-oriented Western theology, the psyche continued to imagine Christian mythology in more holistic terms by giving Mary, the Mother of God, more centrality in practice and iconography. Jung noted with special interest that the figure of Sophia, or personified wisdom, symbolized as female, had even begun to appear in later parts of the Hebrew Bible, thus showing the incorporation even then of a hitherto rejected psychic factor. When in 1950 the Pope proclaimed the Assumption of Mary (i.e., that she was bodily taken to Heaven to join her Son) to be official dogma, Jung took this to represent a *psychological* milestone of considerable importance.

Jung drew attention to the way various Christian subgroups developed the biblical myth toward its fuller psychological implications, albeit outside the bounds of official doctrine. One of these was the Gnostic movement of the second and third centuries. Gnostics ("those who know") claimed a deeper, esoteric knowledge of divinity, typically picturing Christ as "the spiritual inner man," or a principle of light in all humans. At the same time the anthropomorphic creator was often interpreted as a lower, jealous being as opposed to the eternal and higher supreme Wisdom (again personified in female symbolism).

Another Christian subgroup were the alchemists of the late medieval and Renaissance periods. To many alchemists, the process of transforming lead into gold represented a spiritual allegory of transforming humanity into divinity. Even where the symbolism was not deliberate, Jung saw the imageries as a projection onto physical processes of the path of psychological self-realization. The process of alchemy paralleled the process of individuation. From an original chaotic *prima materia*, or raw material (representing to Jung the unformed, untransformed ego), a series of differentiations and reunifications ensued (including stages in which the original substance was blackened, whitened, and reddened—all corresponding to types of psychological transformations). The end result was a refined, divine substance symbolized by such terms as "the philosopher's stone," "Christ," "the mystical marriage of the king and queen," or as gold. These Jung interpreted as symbols of the emergent self.

In these and other mythologies of the reconciliation of psychic opposites, Jung saw attention to a self that had otherwise been split by religious dualisms. In mythologies of the internalization of the divine and the mystical marriage of soul with God, Jung saw the psychological fulfillment of religious systems that had completely dissociated internal and external reality.

Christ as Symbol of the Self. For Jungians, Christ is Western religion's dominant image of the self archetype. Into the figure of Christ—and for other cultures the same may be said of figures like the Buddha—the psyche transposed its ideals. While adherents normally think of Jesus Christ as a supernatural being, to be conceived in terms of doctrine and ritual, the psychologists focus on his role as a symbol of the unconscious psyche.

> He is the still living myth of our culture. He is our culture hero, who, regardless of historical existence, embodies the myth of the divine Primordial Man, the mystic Adam. It is he who occupies the centre of the Christian mandala, who is the lord of the Tetramorph, i.e., the four symbols of the evangelists, which are like the four columns of his throne. He is in us and we in him. His kingdom

is the pearl of great price, the treasure buried in the field, the grain
of mustard seed which will become a great tree, and the heavenly
city.[11]

Psychologically, the question here is not whether Christ was
divine in any historical, objective sense, but how the image of
Christ functions in the believer's psyche as a powerful image of the
self archetype. The relation most people have to Jesus is not as a
historical being but as "one's Lord." Even Saint Paul, the first
great Christian missionary, had never met Jesus in the flesh, but
had been struck in a vision by the impact of Christ as his personal
savior. The first council of bishops in 325 C.E. made an official
declaration that Jesus was not just a historical person but an
eternal form of God. To Jung this all underscored Christ's archetypal nature as an enduring symbol of the self, and as one Jungian
analyst stated, "What the Western man experiences as real when
he participates in the symbol of Christ is only proximately Christ
and ultimately is the Self."[12]

As the "god-man," Christ represents the unity of two parts of
the individual, the self (divine) and the ego (human), and the
incarnation of the former in the latter. He represents the psychological idea that the highest life of the psyche can be found in
selflessness and humility, that great difficulties can be overcome,
that we often take upon ourselves the problems ("sins") of others,
and that there is more to the self than "the judgments of men" and
the standards of "the world." Like Christ, we are all babes born in
the dark of the year, and martyrs for causes not understood by the
ruling powers of society.

It is as the self archetype that Christ comes into the lives of
those who "believe in him." His role as judge, friend, savior,
sacred heart, or suffering servant corresponds to those functions of
the self, as do Christian assurances, like "He understands me
when no one else does," or popular hymns about Jesus as "the
center of my joy," or even as "the laughter that shatters all my
fears." In this way the activation of the self archetype has the
function of "redeeming" fallen egos, giving them a new source of
empowerment.

Nevertheless, Jung thought the image of Christ lacked a
certain human wholeness, because it was understood as being
entirely free of sin, entirely good, and thus as having no dark side.
This therefore became part of the dualistic situation described
above, with its attendant psychological dilemmas. "Only with

Christ did a devil enter the world as the real counterpart of God," notes Jung.[13] Mary, too, born without original sin (according to doctrine), was to become a role model that reinforced the same dichotomy. Combined with the fact that the Christ-image is often conceived as remote, wholly outside ourselves, and supernatural, it remained that the earthy side of the human psyche was left unintegrated.

Asian Religion. Jung's description of the psyche took into account religious concepts from both East and West, though he did see the psychologies of Asian and biblical religions as having significantly different points of emphasis. The first he saw as introverted, placing the highest value on the self as an inner reality; the second as extroverted, intuiting that one is saved only by connection with an outside force and devaluing the role of the ego in redeeming itself. Both reflect psychological truths. Both create psychological dilemmas because of their one-sidedness.

According to Jung, in seeking enlightenment through the transcendence of ego and individuality, Asian religion underrates the world of consciousness, while biblical monotheism in turn underrates the archetype of the inner self. The one values interiority, the other individuality. The one overconnects self and ego, almost obliterating ego, the other underconnects self and ego, almost abandoning ego to its own despair or desperate graspings at outside revelation. The Hindu Upanishads say, "you are That (God, the Supreme Self);" the book of Job asks, "Where were you when I laid the foundation of the earth?" (Job 38:4).

The priority Jung gave to the psychological value of "wholeness" interested him in oriental concepts of the harmony of opposites, e.g., yin and yang. He also found consistent with his ideas certain Hindu or Buddhist concepts that the gods are relative to human spiritual growth and that they "belong to the sphere of illusory separateness and mind-created projections, and yet they exist."[14]

Religious Piety and the Relationship of Ego and Unconscious

Just as Durkheim could not distinguish between gods and society, so Jung found it hard to distinguish between gods and psyche. For Jung the language of myth and the language of the unconscious are two languages representing the same thing. Analogous to Durkheim's society, it is the nature of the psyche to act in a godlike way. The psyche is the witness to all we do. Our ego cannot hide from it. It observes all our faults and promises, all our secrets and private dreams. It is the source, condition, companion, and nemesis of the unfolding of our self-awareness. Like a partner, it acts reciprocally both to the way we face it and to the way we ignore it. It invades us with inspirations and depressions. For better or worse, in the course of time it brings to manifestation the nature and truth of our lives.

The basis of what has traditionally been called religious experience is this relationship of the ego to the underlying self. Prayer is an example. The usual explanation of prayer is either that it refers to a real being "out there" or that it is just talking to the wind—the typical dichotomy created by the rationalism-versus-theology impasse. Like the sociological model in its way, the Jungian frame creates a third alternative that grounds religious experience in a "real" referent, while at the same time agreeing with the rationalist that there may not literally be an entity on the other end of prayer that corresponds exactly to what the believer imagines to be there. The referent is the psyche itself; and any act or attitude of the ego, including religious positionings, affects the total psyche. Nothing we do or desire is unseen, and nothing we say is unheard by this wider unconscious region.

The doctrine that we are sinners savable only by outside grace corresponds to a certain psychological truth. The ego is usually its own problem and cannot "save" itself on its own because of its self-serving motivations. The problem of the ego is its stubborn, self-righteous orientation, which is exactly what must yield for any psychological or spiritual change to take place. In this case it cannot transform itself but must undergo a process of its own dismemberment and reformation. It must let go. It must accept dependence on a higher power—a power which theology calls the grace of God but which Jungian psychology views as the work of the unconscious conspiring with the needs of the ego.[15] Admission of the impossibility of curing itself and of the need for openness to a higher power are therefore often the first, humbling steps toward ego's self-transformation. They are steps which correspond to the message of those forms of religion which preach that we are such sinners that we need Christ (or Buddha, as the case may be) to do for us what we cannot do for ourselves. Similarly, admission of dependency on a higher power is also required in substance addiction programs like Alcoholics Anonymous.

Religion, then, is part of the same psychological process as that enacted in psychotherapy. The relation of soul to god parallels the relationship of patient to therapist: the ego knows it is being heard, understood, evaluated, and accepted. The effectiveness of the process of psychological transformation relates to elements like trust. In conventional, pietistic sayings like "Lord, nothing will happen today that you and I together can't handle," "Lord" is here a symbol of the self as other than the ego, and "I" is the voice of the ego.

The history of religion is filled with accounts of individual "conversions," or sudden feelings of being inwardly changed by an unsolicited, overwhelming religious power. It was in order to explain experiences like this that the philosopher William James, in his *Varieties of Religious Experience* (1901) affirmed the existence of an unconscious part of the self. To James, conversions typically represented a shift from an old self to a newly formed self that had been subliminally incubating in the unconscious, as it were, waiting for its moment to appear. Any outside event could trigger it.

Supernatural voices and visions, too, are explainable by the concept of the unconscious. They represent emotional needs so deep that the psyche fulfills the need. The unconscious itself has the power to create these voices, these other selves, just as it has the power to create alter egos in cases of multiple personality, possession, and trance mediumship. Some concept of a broad and creative unconscious would also seem to be indispensable in interpreting the whole vast world of shamanism, where trance-state "soul travel" and spirit negotiations are culturally normative behavior.

Reflections on the Psychological Frame

Translating religion into psychology was a natural step for a Judeo-Christian culture that became postreligious, scientific, and individualistic all at once.[16] At least the self, the psyche, is real. If the spirits are not out there, at least they are in here. Religion is as real as the psychological realities it represents.

In giving some psychological validity to religious symbols, the Jungian translation of religion—unlike the Freudian one—has had the cultural function of creating a kind of alternative reli-

gious framework. In some ways, intended or not, Jung's interpretations had the effect of producing a metamythology, arrived at
through an almost allegorical method by which religious symbols
become symbols of "the inner journey." Myth is read "outside-
in." The gods are alive after all—within the psyche. The interpretive force of this approach, then, has been more reconstructive
than destructive.

Our interest here has not been in the ambiguities or problems
of particular aspects of Jung's work (e.g., the cross-cultural applicability of the archetypes and their male-oriented character have
both been challenged), but in the force of this general standpoint
as a framework for seeing religion. For while Jung's version of the
gods carries no final scientific authority, it is a striking example of
the applicatory power of an interpretive frame. The general concepts of psyche, the unconscious, and the self have a strong,
extensive explanatory capability in relationship to religious data.

Philosophically, Jung's thought straddled the romanticism of
the nineteenth century, with its desire to find a key to the meaning of symbols, and the relativism of the twentieth, with its
eventual acknowledgement of the constructed nature of all meanings.[17] In the latter regard, Jung's interpretive schema was hedged
with considerable subtlety and reflexivity. In working with pa-
tients, he tried to avoid schematic translations of unconscious
processes into specific meanings, acknowledging that the very
process of determining meanings is relative to the shifting orientations of ego consciousness. Interpretation is less a matter of correct representation and more an act of awareness, part of a
dialogic process by which ego comes to consciousness—part of the
psyche's own history, and not a definition of fixed, objective
truths. The archetype of the self, for example, though it may seem
to "explain" certain religious symbols, is ultimately a conceptual
way of understanding the ego-unconscious relationship, not a
universal religious entity, spirit, or substance in its own right like
the Hindu Atman. Ironically, while Jung did not always see the
European structurings of his own categories, he was keenly aware
of the structured, psychological nature of all thought.

The psychological and sociocultural frames have parallel
functions. The one explains the outer variables of religion, the
other the inner, individual variables. Each accounts for the relativity of religion to setting—the setting of culture or of ego. Each
acknowledges that religious symbols act upon as well as reflect

culture and ego. Each establishes a wide referent—society in the one case, psyche in the other—in order to account for the spectrum of religious data.

Yet because the two approaches scan the data of religion with different detectors, they are not essentially competing for the same turf—just as psychology and physiology are not necessarily mutually exclusive. Again, this is a case of different instruments creating and reading different data.

The sociocultural and psychological frames also have parallel limitations. Most of what can be questioned about the one—the uncertainty of its own ultimate concepts, the totalizing nature of its generalizations, the lack of unity within the field—can be questioned of the other.

Like all organisms (and sociologists), psychologists too fashion worlds in their own image. The ultimate difference between the views of Freud and Jung was not in empirical data but in the two psychologists' own biographical horizons, their resultant motivations, and their subsequent controlling models of the self. For the rationalist Freud, psychoanalysis and religion were necessarily irreconcilable. Psychological understanding was a step out of the muddy waters of superstition and self-deception. Jung, in contrast, was struck by the problem of the overrationalization of the ego such that it became insensitive to the need for inner adjustments. He was impressed with the dilemma that the rational ego, which to Freud was an achievement, creates its own problems of one-sidedness, neglect, and willfulness that in turn need resolution through a more holistic cooperation with the transrational unconscious. Religious images, like dreams, are often a healing, mediating symbolism by which this adjustment is made. And if religious experience is an illusion, Jung countered Freud, it is a "very real illusion." "What is the difference between a real illusion," Jung asked, "and a healing religious experience? It is merely a difference in words."[18]

Like sociologies, then, the many psychologies do not agree on specific explanatory models. They differ in what they take the self to be. Are the gods ciphers of our narcissistic power? Of our sexuality? Of our suffering? Is it ecstatic Dionysius or balanced Apollo that rules the self? And what about "the goddesses within?" What is the difference between a woman's and a man's self? The extensions of Freudian, humanistic, and transpersonal psychologies, and neo-Jungian archetypal psychology[19]—reveal an inexhaustible spectrum of possible paradigms for understanding selfhood.

Yet there is still another way to understand religion. What would religion look like if it were to be seen as a subject matter in its own right, in terms of its own comparative categories, without either theological purposes on the one hand or sociopsychological purposes on the other? What does "comparative religion" have to say about religion, and what does it see that other approaches do not?

5

Comparative Perspective in the Study of Religion

There is another interpretive framework which looks at religion as a subject matter that can be understood in terms of its own comparative patterns. Originally called "the science of religion," and later "comparative religion," the "history and phenomenology of religion," or even "religious studies," it differentiated itself from theology as well as sociological and psychological systems of explanation, creating a descriptive ground of its own.[1] The premises of comparative religion are that religion is a worldwide form of culture that needs to be understood before it is explained, and that to understand it means to know its cross-cultural patterns and varieties in balanced perspective. The parts can then be seen in relation to the whole, variations in relation to themes, and innovations in relation to global historical patterns. Thus, one cannot fully understand a god, savior, or creation myth without comprehending the whole range of gods, saviors, and creation myths.

The idea of interpreting religion as a modern subject matter for study alongside other human sciences was a nineteenth-century creation, made possible primarily by the emergent knowledge of Asian religions. In the 1860s the German-born Oxford scholar F. Max Müller began calling for a "science of religion" that would approach the subject not in the previous fashion of speculative theories, but on the basis of accurate information about non-Western traditions and evenhanded comparisons between all types of religions.[2] Because it was grounded in an

impartial, unbiased attitude toward the data, he likened it to the
new study of geology and other sciences that were now to be
inductively accountable to facts rather than based on deductions
from a particular religious ideology. Religion was to become a
subject that could be examined and generalized about independently of the churches, and no longer used just to illustrate precon-
ceived philosophies that had no sense of religion's global history.
The science of religion was to be based on sound comparative
study of all religions, and Müller's claim became, "He who knows
one, knows none."[3] If we only know one, we do not know what it
has in common with the others, and therefore we do not know
what is different about it.

Previous to this new comparative and historical outlook, religion had been studied only through the frames of religious beliefs,
and ignorance about religions other than the Judeo-Christian
traditions was profound. As recently as the beginning of the
1800s, the standard Western classification of all religions could
identify only four main types: Christianity, Judaism, Islam, and a
catchall category labeled "paganism," implying that all peoples of
other religions outside the light of monotheism were heathens
who worshiped false gods. Knowledge of the great traditions of the
East helped bring an end to this artificial and prejudicial schema.

The rise of comparative religion therefore coincided with the
deprovincializing of Western thought, for most of what had gone
under the name of "the philosophy of religion" had equated
religion with Western religion. The presence of non-Western
spiritual universes and of genres of religion different than the
biblical types, and the scholars' attitudes of respect for them, put a
whole new light on the question of the nature of religion and
challenged traditional Western stereotypes about it.

The new, objective study of religion became a field of research
in universities and has remained so to this day, having undergone numerous transformations. Departments of religious studies,
with no connection at all to any religious institutions, are now
a normal part of university scholarship and education, and coexist alongside departments of sociology, anthropology, and
psychology.

Though the field is still in process of development, this chapter attempts an overall, synthetic picture of how the comparative
approach differs from others and what its essential interpretive
model contributes.

Religion as a Subject Matter

The typical modern representative of the comparative viewpoint is Mircea Eliade (1907–86), a Romanian scholar who taught in the United States and whose works and terminology became highly influential.[4] While Eliade's work sometimes contains philosophical values that go beyond a wholly objective, comparative approach, most of the time it consistently embodies the main ingredients of the model we are considering here. "The ultimate aim of the historian of religion," Eliade summarizes, "is to understand, and to make understandable to others, religious man's behavior and mental universe."[5] The viewpoints of the believers become the data of cross-cultural study.

Eliade advocated that religious expressions, like artistic expressions, should be understood at their own level, that is, in terms of their own unique ways of structuring experience. He writes in a well-known passage,

> Every religious experience is expressed and transmitted in a particular historical context. But admitting the historicity of religious experiences does not imply that they are reducible to non-religious forms of behavior. Stating that a religious datum is always a historical datum does not mean that it is reducible to a non-religious history—for example, to an economic, social, or political history. We must never lose sight of one of the fundamental principles of modern science: *the scale creates the phenomenon.* . . . Henri Poincaré asked, not without irony, "Would a naturalist who had never studied the elephant except through the microscope consider that he had an adequate knowledge of the creature?" The microscope reveals the structure and mechanism of cells, which structure and mechanism are exactly the same in all multicellular organisms. The elephant is certainly a multicellular organism, but is that all that it is? On the microscopic scale, we might hesitate to answer. On the scale of human vision, which at least has the advantage of presenting the elephant as a zoölogical phenomenon, there can be no doubt about the reply.[6]

Eliade admits that "obviously there are no *purely* religious phenomena," and that "because religion is human it must for that very reason be something social, something linguistic, something economic—you cannot think of man apart from language and society."[7] But he avers that it is as hopeless to think that religion is fully explained by these approaches as it is to think that a work of art could be so explained.

Religion, like the arts, *can* be explained from the viewpoint of other fields, but like them it can also be investigated and understood in terms of its own way of viewing the world. We can study music not just as a product of society or culture, but in terms of music itself (rhythm, harmony, and so on)—and the same goes for art and literature. Like the arts, it is the nature of religion to configure experience through its own expressive and imprinting categories of language and behavior. Thus we should study religions not only in terms of their social contexts, but also in terms of their own religious visions. It is incumbent on the historian of religions, Eliade advocates, to bring out the experienced religious "values" of religion, the point of view of the believer—for as a universal part of human culture, systems of religious symbols have dominated and inspired human life for centuries.

Religion in this sense—as an active viewpoint of believers— is not just an expression of society but a creator of society. Its language and behavior make the world over into its own patterns. It defines and shapes worlds. It not only posits a world view, but inhabits it and acts it out. From religion come conceptions of history, time, space, cosmology, nature, and human nature. More than the arts, which are temporary enclaves of imagination, religions generate what might be called enduring, even timeless models of reality. That is, religious language does not present itself as fantasy or imagination but as a description of that on which the world is really grounded. It sets down the standards of behavior, and institutionalizes the power to back up its claims and render them plausible and viable. So while religion is like art in that it has its own language, it is also parallel to government and even science in the way its language functions as an institutionally based law of the land and a map of reality. Religion complexly involves both imagery and commitment.

The Language of Religion. Religion has its own forms of expression, and it is these forms that make it religion rather than science or government. Part of Eliade's contribution was to draw attention to the way religion expresses itself through the languages of myth, symbol, and ritual, and to show how religiousness can be understood as a way of experiencing the world through these categories. For example, religion gives value and meaning to actions and objects in the world by seeing them *in terms of* mythic prototypes.

Religious language in its primary sense is participatory and invocative rather than empirical and detached. It is language which grounds human action in images about the nature of the world and which is exemplified in scriptures or their oral equivalents. Unlike scientific language, which by its nature is nonsubjective and nonparticipatory, religious language connects individuals with a moral order, offering stories, teachings, and images about the meaning or purpose of life, and giving guidelines for behavior that correspond to them. Religious language is not just an explanation of the world—science does that too—but a way, for its adherents, of *inhabiting* the world. This habitative function means that religious people see the world through the lens of mythic or scriptural vocabularies and regulate their lives according to the models and injunctions set forth in such traditions. They rest on the Sabbath because God did, exercise love and compassion because Jesus or the Buddha did, observe the Ten Commandments because people were enjoined to do so in the great time of the Mount Sinai revelation, or practice selfless action because Krishna so taught in the immortal words of the Bhagavad Gita.

Here is language endowed with the prestige of primal, divine status and origins, with the power of creation, the memory of founding ancestors, and the wisdom of great beings like Buddha, Christ, or Confucius. Religious words are of such sacred authority that followers live and die by them.

Religion is therefore an entirely different system of language than science, and the two systems clearly describe different parts of the human universe.

Sacred ritual is also an important part of the language of religion. We have seen how it can be explained sociologically, but it can also be viewed as a vehicle of religious expression in its own right. For example, the enactment of the Sacrifice of Christ may have a sociological or even psychological meaning, but it also has a participatory, religious meaning for the believer—a religious as well as a social function. It may consolidate group feelings, but it also imprints and transforms the group feelings with supernatural images. One of the great functions of ritual is to enact the *content* of religious or mythic truths.

Religion and the Sacred. For comparativists like Eliade, religion is about *the sacred,* just as for Durkheimians it is about society, and for Jungians it is about the psyche. What does it mean to say that religion is a system of language and practices which organizes the world around what is deemed sacred?

In this context *the sacred* refers to those focal objects which to the insider seem endowed with superhuman power and authority. Depending on the culture, it could be a scripture, a great person or high religious leader, a god, an ancestor, an institution like the Catholic Church, an aspect of nature such as a mountain or river, a path of discipline taught by a Buddha, or a sacred rite. These objects, words, beings, and observances are charged with a power that governs, inspires, and obliges the life of participants. Any object can become a vehicle of sacred power. Any religion is a system of ways of experiencing the sacred, that is, objects which convey superhuman meaning.

The element of the sacred can be understood from two angles. In the first place, it is a supernatural value placed on something. In this sense the sacred is that set of things that any humans at any time or place have held in inviolable esteem. In the second place, it is a power by which humans feel encountered, a power experienced as other, real, divine, and mysterious. It is, as experienced by participants, an extraordinary force, like a god. So from the point of view of comparative religious studies, sacredness is both a way of constructing the world and a way that objects are felt to act upon the adherents. It is both a value given to objects (a value manifested in behavior toward the objects) and an awesome experience *of* those objects (experienced as openings to or from another, transcendent realm).

In this way *the sacred* is a term drawn from the world of religion, but generalized to refer to the overarching common denominator of all religious life. Other expressions, like "experience of the supernatural," "encounter with the holy," "feeling of the numinous," or "sense of the transcendent" have also been used. Strictly speaking, *the sacred* is just a descriptive category, and the use of the term in comparative religion neither affirms nor denies that there is a superhuman reality behind it. The value of the term is its faithful approximation of the character of religious experience and behavior, and the way in which it can be understood to have different kinds of content (that is, any number of kinds of things can be sacred to someone). Where there is belief in something holy, humans act differently; this comparative religion describes, while at the same time showing that the types of things that *are* sacred will vary significantly among cultures.

The concept of the sacred thus becomes an instrument of understanding worlds other than one's own. It draws attention to the focal point around which other peoples' religious life forms, and understanding this renders their behavior and language more intelligible. If we see what it is that is sacred in the mind of the believer, then we align ourselves in a way that corresponds to his or her worldview. Sacred things are so because of the immense role they play and the absolute priority they have in someone's world. To miss that role is to miss the point of the behavior, since what is sacred functions as what is "real." Because sacredness is always embodied in particular forms, students of comparative religion are expected to see that it is not the literal, surface aspect of the forms or objects that are revered, but the transhuman force or sacredness felt *in* them.

There are thousands of systems of sacred things, just as there are thousands of kinds of works of art. The different things in which sacredness is embodied, the different behaviors connected with them, the different transformations holiness has undergone, and above all the different worlds it forms, constitute here the history of religion and the subject matter of comparative description.

Suspension of Judgment. As a descriptive enterprise, the comparative study of religion tries to proceed without the interpretive bias of any particular religious or antireligious position. Rather than looking at religion as something right or wrong, it looks at it as a *type* of experience, behavior, and symbol system. Religion is therefore seen as a *phenomenon.* This method is analogous to the way a zoologist would look at a species, or a literary historian at the works of an author. People *do* experience the world in religious terms. *That* they do it and *how* they do it can be examined and compared without recourse to explanations about what causes religion or what reality lies behind it. If some people experience the world in terms of Catholic ideas and others experience it in terms of Confucian ideas, these are facts that can be investigated and understood, and one does not need to accept those ideas in order to describe them. To the comparativist, religious beliefs are first of all expressions of someone's worldview rather than propositions to be argued in terms of their independent truth.

The comparative attitude therefore calls for a dispassionate capacity to comprehend and explain other people's experience of their worlds without interjecting one's own preferences. One must "bracket off" one's own concepts of how the world ought to be organized in order to listen to how others configure it, and temporarily set aside what the world means to oneself in order to gain access to what the world means to others.

This attitude of modern comparative religion may be initially hard to grasp, because on the surface religion seems specifically to be about certain claims to truth. We live in a rationalist culture that questions the truth of biblical assertions vis à vis our culture's own empirical knowledge, and it is natural to look at other religions in terms of their parallel claims. Stepping back from the issue of whether religious ideas are valid and observing religious thought as a behavioral phenomenon is not always a natural step to take, yet it is precisely the comparative viewpoint. To continue Eliade's metaphor, when the naturalist studies elephants, no one thinks, "Is the elephant right or is it wrong?" When the geologist studies rocks, no one thinks, "Are the rocks right or are they wrong?" In comparative religious studies the rocks and the elephants are people's sacred beliefs and practices. Different symbol systems about gods, different observances of worship or meditation—these are "the facts" whose functions in life are to be understood.

And a large part of understanding them involves comparing them.

Comparative Perspective. If religion is a subject matter, it is not just a series of isolated facts, but a series of facts that relate to each other in terms of similarities and differences, patterns and innovations. As a subject matter, the parts need to be understood in relation to the whole, and the whole in terms of the parts. This is why one of the first tasks of nineteenth-century science of religion was to create accurate typologies of religion, much like taxonomic classifications of species in botanical science. Inventories of patterns common to different religions also began, showing the prevalence of themes like sacrifice, creation myths, and purification rites.

The study of religious patterns is sometimes referred to as the "phenomenology of religion." The word *phenomenon* literally means something "observable" (from the Greek *phainomena*, "appearance"). Phenomenology is the study of things in their observable aspects as opposed to their causality, and the term has that meaning in the sciences as well as in religion. The "phenomenology of religion" first became a name for this classificatory phase of study, and later was given fuller meaning by including in it the principles and process of *understanding* religious phenomena.[8]

For comparison is not simply a matter of classification, but ultimately a tool of understanding. Each religious world is different and yet has things in common with others. Christian theology, for example, cannot fathom its own uniqueness if it does not know which of its parts belong to religion in general and which are distinctively its own. Hinduism also speaks about incarnations of God, and some forms of Buddhism include beliefs in a great Buddha who will deliver us from sin if we accept him in faith. Moreover, much that might otherwise be obscure or unintelligible in religion is often illuminated by understanding its generic functions and patterns.

Of course, the committed insider might not wish to see things in this lateral fashion. The believer usually assumes his or her own religion to be unique and sufficient. One's needs for religious knowledge do not go beyond it—it is all one needs to know. Its forms are not seen as variations of universal patterns but as singular, self-contained revelations. Readers of *The Varieties of Religious Experience* will recall William James's comment that "probably a crab would be filled with a sense of personal outrage if it could hear us class it without ado or apology as a crustacean, and thus dispose of it. 'I am no such thing,' it would say; 'I am MYSELF, MYSELF alone.' "[9] The crab's view is the insider's view, and the crab does not need to hear about crustaceans. Its membership is local. It sees itself as a citizen of a species ("I'm a Baptist," or "I'm a Muslim"), not of a vague religious genus, family, or kingdom. Devotees might not want to hear or know that their gods, holy days, scriptures, or rites are versions of global, cross-cultural patterns.

But that is the task of the comparative perspective—to look beyond the private claims of all particular religions and see the whole set in terms of continuities and differences. The remainder of the chapter will illustrate this process.

The Comparative Process: The Interplay of Similarity and Difference

Comparative perspective does not mean that interpretation stops once one has found a pattern of similarity or difference. The comparative frame aims at understanding any particular religious expression better by virtue of knowing the pattern of which it is an illustration. The rationale is that the more we know about a subject, the better we can grasp any particular aspect of it. Knowledge about one religion throws light on another. Familiarity with the patterns and functions of ritual can clarify a particular instance of ritual that might not otherwise make sense. Familiarity with the history and patterns of conceiving divinity can show any one version of a god in the exact context of its relationship to all the other versions. Only familiarity with the history of religious traditions and patterns can show us what is innovative about them. In this way the data of religion become mutually edifying. The comparative perspective builds a context for interpreting religious life, providing an "educated," resonant matrix of associations and patternings that has itself been derived from a study of the different traditions.

This comparative process is present in all fields of knowledge. You know less about your computer, your car, or your cat if you know nothing about other kinds of computers, other kinds of cars, or other kinds of cats. You do not know what *kind* of computer, car, or cat you have. You do not know what others of their kind have that yours does not, and you do not know what yours has that others do not.

The analogy goes further. If you have never seen any animals other than a cat, and your language has no words or categories for any others, then it may be hard to understand dogs, fish, or zebras other than as odd versions of cats—as large cats, furless cats without legs that swim, and giant ugly cats with stripes. Similarly, in times when we had no categories for other religions, and had only blanket, negative classifications like "paganism," it was hard to see Buddhists and Hindus as other than people who worshiped false gods.

Even within the sciences, comparison (though the word itself may not be used) is the very heart of the process of knowledge. We know what a thing is by differentiating its properties from others, whether it is a subatomic particle or a type of nebula. Understanding cross-cultural patterns in religion is something like understanding the chart of the physical elements in chemistry. Knowing the basic "values" of or differences between elements makes it possible to understand compounds and combinations, and makes it easier to not confuse or judge the characteristic activity of one chemical element by the standards of another.

The comparative process therefore moves back and forth between understanding particulars through their commonality with a pattern, and appreciating particulars through their difference from other variations on a pattern. Comparative perspective means seeing both similarity and difference.

Understanding Patterns. The language of religion is usually highly specific. To the insider, specific gods, words, objects, and observances are absolute, as in "Jesus is Lord," "the Holy Qur'an," or reference to a mountain in Bali, Gunung Agung, as "the center of the universe." Without any comparative understanding, it may be difficult to know what to make of such particularistic claims. To outsiders they will seem either wrong, threatening, presumptuous, odd, or unintelligible. Here is exactly where the comparative perspective comes in.

It is a common function of religion to approach the absolute through the specific. Buddha, Krishna, and Christ are *all* "the Lord;" the Lotus Sutra, the Torah, and the Qur'an are *all* holy scripture; the Zuni Mountains in New Mexico, the Kaaba in Mecca, and Gunung Agung in Bali are *all* "the center of the world." The series of things that function as lords and saviors, as scriptures, and as centers of the world can be studied as sets, as variations on a theme. They are patterned ways in which people give focus to the sacred and thus to their world. The very multiplicity of sacred centers, texts, and objects underscores the normalcy of the activity of constructing the world in these ways. The thousands of "origins of the world," if taken as literal claims to objective truth, as rationalism would do, would indeed result in a chaos of mutual contradictions.

The patterns are endless. Every tradition has specific words and behaviors that may seem to be one-of-a-kind to the insider, but which from a global perspective are seen to share similar functions with their counterparts in other religions. Buddha's enlightenment, Jesus's resurrection, and Muhammed's reception of the Qur'an are all "the supreme event in history." Easter, the Chinese New Year's Eve, and the Muslim Night of Power during Ramadan are all "the holiest time of the year." It could even be said that any religious symbol system functions as the universe itself, as "the order of things."

The saying that "you can't compare apples and oranges" expresses the truth that you can't compare things that are essentially different. At one level, religions may seem just too historically unique to compare. But what might appear discrepant on one plane could be related and continuous on other levels. Botanically, apples and oranges are both fruits, two among hundreds of species of that genus. As such they have a great deal in common, and far from being incomparable they are in the larger picture minor variations on the same thing. Likewise, Buddhism and Christianity may seem to be different in surface features, but "botanically," i.e., in terms of comparative religion, they are both religions (the same genus) and have a great deal in common.

Once the continuities of function are grasped, once we know to what pattern or place a religious expression belongs, the strangeness of religions may become not so strange. What would otherwise remain inscrutable, bizarre, or foreign might turn out to be part of a common pattern of human behavior. The literal, highly specific, surface content of religion might no longer obscure its common function.

Understanding Differences. The weight of emphasis on pattern or difference will vary according to the analytical or even educational needs at hand. Things cannot be different, of course, unless they have something in common. Apples, oranges, avocados, and pineapples may all be fruits and in that sense "the same," but they are conceivably even more interesting for their differences. Chess and football are both games, but their contrasts are more pertinent to us than their similarities. Tricycles and jets are both transportation, but no one would confuse them in planning a trip. Whales, bobcats, and humans are all species of the genus mammal, but their similarities are of concern only to specialists in comparative zoology. Gunung Agung in Bali and the Kaaba in Mecca are both cosmic centers, but their differences are at least as important as their analogies.

Once the common theme is of interest, interest in the variations is heightened. If we are interested in knee injuries, hair styles, or rock music, then the varieties of those themes automatically become objects of concern if not fascination. Where a theme emerges, then the variations themselves give richness to the theme, just as in the use of the theme and variations form in music. By the time a musical theme has been expressed in different major and minor keys and in different tempos and moods, it comes back at the end more impressively than in its simple statement at the beginning. We then hear the theme more fully because we hear it in terms of its variations—all the different things the theme has been and can be. It is this way in the comparative approach to religion, too.

Difference, like similarity, exists at all levels of religion. There are different types of religious systems in general, different kinds of content in religious teachings, different kinds of religious "purity." In an important sense every religious system (like every person), is a unique configuration of cultural and historical elements, and as a whole is different from every other system. Not only are religious worlds not the same, but at every moment in the life of a religious individual or community the religious setting is different from that of every other such moment. Likewise, the same image or act, like "heaven" or burial, may have a different value or meaning according to its role in different cultures.

In referring to similarities, examples were given of common functions, such as ways that the "center of the world" symbol may operate to orient and focus a universe. But *what* the center is is another matter. Here is the question of the content rather than the function of religion.

All religions name the forces that ground the world. This is a common activity. Mythologizing the origins of the world has a similar function everywhere—that of relating one's world to the forces upon which it depends and giving those forces paradigmatic status. Yet in spite of these similarities, the origin myths speak of very different kinds of forces and kinds of worlds. If we were made in the image of God, in which god's image was it? Or was it not in a god's image at all? Early Buddhism says that the world is a projection of the mind's own ignorance. The religious differences here are obviously crucial. Religions have varying images of reality itself. In one tradition "the world" is a contest of love and hate; in another a negotiation of yin and yang; in another an extension of either wisdom or ignorance. "The world" may be the result of a power struggle, divine fiat, procreation, ignorance, sacrifice, or divine kingship.

All religious worlds periodically renew themselves through focused observances. Again, these rites may have the similar function of regenerating the vitality of the sacred. But what is the sacred thing that is observed and renewed on these occasions? Is it a contractual relation to neighboring tribes? Personal rebirth? States of meditation? The prowess of warriors? Respect for one's patron saint? Filial piety? The prestige of the king? Ethnic or gender empowerment? Precisely because comparative religion understands the common function, it is then able to pay attention to these different values showcased by the innumerable festivals and rites of renewal.

All religious worlds draw lines between moral and immoral behavior. But what is it, exactly, that is deemed negative, profane or evil? The nature of sin, pollution, and negativity also vary with different worlds. In one it may be promiscuity, in another pride, and in another selfishness, uncleanness, or even laziness. The distinction of pure and impure may be external and ritualistic, or it may be internal and mystical, all-important differences.

Diversity, then, is central to comparative understanding. While religions may all share in the ongoing human activity of world fashioning, each creates a different world—each, as Eliade emphasized, introduces new meanings and values into common religious structures.

Typologies: Different Kinds of Religion

Religions are not all of one type. Religious life paradoxically contains its own opposite types. It is both otherworldly and this-worldly; contemplative and ecstatic; the worship of "the Other" and the discovery of the self; an outgoing, ethical act, and an inward, gathering act; a moment of prophetic rebellion and a moment of quiet propriety. For every specific activity or world-view with which religion has been equated, there is an opposite type of activity or worldview that has also been associated with it. One of the reasons there are so many conflicting theories of religion is that there are so many disparate types or modes of religiousness with which they match up.

Therefore in attempting to do justice to the sheer variety of religious life, comparative religion not only identifies common functions and patterns, but also acknowledges typologies of kinds of religious cultures.

Classifications can all too easily reflect distinctions that serve the religious interests of the classifiers. Christians, as we shall see, produce Christian typologies. Buddhists produce Buddhist typologies. Since the nineteenth century, monotheistic interpretations of the evolution of religion often identified three stages of history and faith—animism, polytheism, and monotheism—suggesting an evolutionary, progressive hierarchy. Even when Asian religion came into more prominence and could no longer be labeled "paganism," Christian interpreters tended to stereotype it as a "world-denying" as opposed to a "creation-affirming" (i.e., Christian) type of religious system. Other Western classifications distinguish nature religions and ethical religions; religions of rit-ual and religions of faith or love; religions of history and cosmic religions. Often these classifications have a judgmental tone.

The comparative study of religion ideally typologizes in the interests of understanding rather than of ideology. While it can never be completely free from interpretive bias, and its distinc-tions will always be an interested selection from an endless amount of data, it nevertheless pursues accuracy and objectivity in the clarification of difference within the world of religion. Ideally, typologies call attention to distinctive religious outlooks by virtue of their contrastive juxtapositions. The nature of one kind of religious expression is made explicit by highlighting its difference from another type. Typologies are here hypotheses to be explored, rather than religious affirmations to be defended.

Religious types can be created around any theme. There are types of views of reality (e.g., monism, dualism); types of religious organization (e.g., sects, churches); types of membership (e.g., world, ethnic, or local religions); types of religious experience (mysticism, shamanism, possession); and so on. The following illustration shows types of value-orientations among some of the great religious traditions.

Types of Major Religious Traditions. For beginning students, one of the most useful and important classifications is between Asian and biblical traditions. Modern comparative perspective here makes no attempt to defend biblical religion as the norm, but looks at it as a *type* of religion among others. Among the larger religious traditions, three important groupings can be identified: (1) reli-gions of biblical origin, (2) religions originating in India (e.g., Hinduism and Buddhism), and (3) East Asian religions (e.g., Confucianism and Taoism).

From the point of view of global religious history, the biblical type of religion originating in Palestine is quite distinct in content from those deriving from India and China. It embraces Judaism, Christianity, and Islam with all their offshoots, and has as its common base the image of God presented in the Hebrew Bible. Judaism is the oldest, "mother" religion here, but both Chris-tianity and Islam see themselves as direct continuations of the Jewish religious vision. Islam (founded in 622 C.E.) views Mu-hammed (570–632 C.E.) as the last of the Prophets, who included Moses and Jesus, and sees the Holy Qur'an as the final communication of God, after the Jewish Torah and Christian Gospels. So these three monotheisms are historically or genetically cousins, and together they form branches of the tree of biblical religion.

The common elements of this tradition are the beliefs that (1) there is a supreme being who is the creator and moral overseer of life and history; (2) the highest human activity is the worship and obedience of this god; (3) there is a radical difference between God and humans, the creator and the creation; (4) God has opened up communication with humanity through special historical emissaries (Abraham, Moses, Jesus, and Muhammed); (5) the will and nature of God has been decisively communicated to humans through the words set down in holy scripture; (6) the focus of morality is the care for others; and (7) the above truths are historically embodied in a special religious community ordained by God as the vehicle of his truths (Judaism, Christianity, and Islam).

The Hindu-Buddhist type, by contrast, represents the "India tree" and its fields of influence, wholly independent of biblical ideas and having its own configuration of religious values. Here there is a prominent pattern in which the world is understood as an interplay of relative, limited, illusory human perception on the one hand and eternal, cosmic truth on the other. This interplay is found in every human being, whose real identity, hidden behind the ignorance of outward life, is ultimately conjoined with divinity (Hinduism) or Buddhahood (Buddhism). In this outlook, the ultimate paradigm of religiousness is not worship or moral obedience (although these play a definite role in popular Hinduism and Buddhism), but the inward discipline of finding the path to an enlightened realization of the deeper truth of one's life.

A third type of tradition, rooted in East Asia, is again quite different. The primary image of religiousness native to China, Korea, and Japan is harmoniousness with the given, natural order of the world. The prime spiritual value is thus to behave in appropriate, fitting relationship to the world and its Tao (or "way"). Taoism conceives this in terms of metaphors of nature, Confucianism in terms of social relationships and virtues. Right relationship, then, is the highest value—not salvation, or worship of God, or liberation from material attachments. The embodiment of East Asian religiousness is not the saint but the sage. The eternal Tao of things is known through seasoned wisdom and the cultivation of character.

So here in these three very general world outlooks—and we have not even mentioned African, Native American, and other traditional cultures—we find significant differences in the content and style of religiousness. Each has its own self-contained religious logic, and each has paths commensurate with its goals and visions. In modern terms they are like different computer programs or software systems—containing varying purposes and instructions. Depending on which of these models forms our starting point—the worship of God, self-liberation, or harmony with nature or society—our interpretation of "religion" varies dramatically, and it is for this reason that Western philosophies of religion have been limited for so long by lack of a genuinely comparative base of understanding.

Reflections on the Comparative Frame

Comparative religion, through the act of describing this multitude of religious situations, creates a kind of interpretive frame of its own. When Eliade says the aim of the historian of religions is "to decipher and explicate every kind of encounter of man with the sacred, from prehistory to our day,"[10] he is presenting a broad, alternative format for viewing the subject, and putting a new vocabulary in play. The universal forms and functions of religion become the matrix of perceiving any religious phenomenon—and any religious act or symbol is viewed as an instance of the general phenomenon of religion.

Comparative religion thus views religion itself as a way of seeing, a form of world construction. Religion here does not just represent a social force or a psychological situation, but a way of interpreting experience through its own symbolisms. The lens of comparative religion thus includes the idea that religion is itself a lens that re-creates and transfigures the perceptual world.

Yet the comparative approach, too, has its limitations, and has drawn criticism on several counts.

The first criticism is the argument that in spite of any neutral guise, there is no such thing as pure description or objectivity in the study of religion, nor is there any such thing as pure understanding. Description always takes place in terms of an interpretive framework that has some motivated cultural or philosophical agenda. Understanding always occurs in terms of some conceptual horizon. Comparison is always a purposive selection of data from an endless array of possible things to compare.

To be sure, the comparative method has historically been connected with quite different agendas. It has been used as an instrument to show the superiority of one religion over others, or as a weapon against the claims of any one religion, or as an attempt to prove that all religions are really the same. Even the modern, so-called neutral comparative study of religion has not been without its own philosophical contexts. Eliade, for example, believed that comparative religion had a cultural role to perform that would be like a second Renaissance, allowing new, non-Western ideas to creatively influence Western culture and self-understanding. He was also concerned that secular culture had lost the sense of the sacred altogether, and thus had something to learn from traditional, cosmically oriented worldviews. He has been criticized by other historians of religion for speaking of the sacred as though it were an actual spiritual reality manifested through time and culture.[11] It is certainly the case that in showing alternatives to secular, nonreligious ways of construing the world, and in providing a rationale for the function of religious symbols, Eliade has appeared to many as an advocate of the recovery of sacred values.

While there does not seem to be any absolutely value-free, objective way to characterize the patterns and structures of religion, the comparative framework nevertheless justifies its approach as a corrective both to uninformed or provincial ideas of religion, and to stances that view religion only in terms of its social and psychological functions.

A second criticism of the comparative approach is that, by relating every religious phenomenon to a type or pattern, it misses elements of historical uniqueness and contextual meaning.[12] We have also seen this problem in the previous chapters. The analogy would be that of trying to describe a specific human individual only through similarity or difference with standard personality types. Such a net misses the specific configurative circumstances of the actual person. Yet religious behavior is always the behavior of specific persons at specific times, within the context of specific worlds. In a world where no two people, or even two cells, are exactly alike, the significance of the historical particularity of religious life might seem to remain elusively off the comparative grid.

While this criticism has force, still we have seen that in looking at differences as well as similarities, comparative work does not entirely neglect specificity. If the pattern at hand is something as broad as "worlds," then each "world" must be studied on its own contextual terms as well as in its commonalities. Every world or person is indeed unique, but every world or person is also a *version* of a world or person. So differences, versions, nuances—or as Eliade liked to say, "innovations"—are at least in principle acknowledged and accommodated in the comparative perspective. In any case, a combination of the comparative perspective plus close ethnographic and historical examination of detail would seem to be a possible direction that would ultimately meet this criticism. We shall investigate later (chapter 7) how a religious expression is many different things, according to what it means to different people, or even to the same person in different circumstances. The comparative framework ideally ought to be able to account for this variety and specificity, rather than snuff it out by clamping timeless, rigid typologies on it. At the same time, not all patterns are universal, and the work of differentiating global from regional and local patterns is a task still in need of much refinement. [13]

Another criticism of comparativism asks, What if there is no such thing as religion in any generic sense? What if it is only an invention, a word made up to justify a certain interpretive approach? And if so, isn't it illusory to speak about "it"—which does not really exist—having patterns, having an anatomy, having manifestations, and so on? And the same could be asked about the phrase *the sacred.* Doesn't the validity of comparative religion beg the question of the validity of *religion* as a reality?

The challenge would be most acute if the word *religion* was indeed being used to represent more than a conceptual classification of various phenomena, and instead was being used as an explanation or cause of the existence of those phenomena, as though the term represented some reified, transcendent force behind them. Yet the comparative perspective, strictly speaking, does not depend on any reference to the independent reality of the sacred. It notes that there is a certain range of human behavior—various ways of experiencing the world in terms of sacredness—and gives a name to this, just as one might note gulls, robins, crows, sparrows, and other feathered creatures that fly and call them *birds. Birds* here has only a classificatory existence. The term exists only through its particular embodiments, and in order to differentiate one type of animal from others, e.g., from fish and mammals. In the same way, religion is a class of behavior and a symbol system that can usefully be differentiated from others. Naturally it is not as clearly definable as a class of animal species. It demarks a general area—not a precise, exclusive territory—to be explored.[14]

We recall that the same question has been asked about the terms *society* and *psyche,* and it has also been put to those who speak about *art* or *economics.* Like these other verbal entities, *religion* can have either an explanatory or descriptive slant, depending on the purposes of its user.

Finally, there is the criticism that the comparative approach has nothing to say about the truth and validity of religion or about what it *ought* to be. It seems to have no evaluative capacity, no capacity to judge worth. It seems hopelessly democratic.

This would seem to be a fair enough point, though it is not necessarily a criticism: different lenses do different things, and evaluative pronouncements are not things this lens does. At the same time that it eschews—or abdicates—judgment, the comparative perspective shifts interpretive focus to a different kind of concept, namely understanding.

There is one more significant viewpoint to be presented here that does indeed deal with forthright judgment. It is the interpretive positions of insiders—religious lenses themselves. These quite definitely take the evaluation of religion and religious truth as their task. They represent not only major historical positions on the spectrum of interpretive frames, but also prime examples of how the act of framing works.

6

Religious Interpretations of Religion: Views from the Inside

Religion is not just inarticulate, passive, unconscious of itself, or available only for outsiders to interpret. Religion has a voice of its own. It too is an interpreter of religion. The voices of insiders are included here not because in them we now finally arrive at the unreduced truth, but because in them we find still another type of viewing lens alongside the others. Religious discourse here takes its place among a host of ways of speaking about the world, and is not just relegated to being the "nonscientific" way that somehow stands outside all the other normal, naturalistic explanations of the way things are. All views, as we have seen, are filters.

The Lens of Religious Language

For adherents, the truths of their religion are the ultimate lenses by which they see themselves and their universe. Religious interpretation assumes its stance directly and faithfully from its own religious language. All that it has to say derives from its own vocabulary and texts, its own gods. It sees the world through its Christs, its Buddhas, and its Qur'ans, and is ultimately limited only by the extent of its own religious understanding and imagination.

Interpretation here is not merely theory, but an act of faith, an act of fathoming what is given in one's tradition as holy and most real. If religiousness is an activity, a type of behavior, then religious interpretation is a form of that activity. Insiders are not persons who have a theory about religion and then decide that they will become believers. Rather, they have a theory about religion because they are believers. We can speak of the gods, the Christian theologian Paul Tillich wrote, only on the basis of our relation to them.[1] Buddhist exegetes affirm that "enlightenment provides the ultimate criterion for interpretation."[2]

Religious interpretation has many functions, and among them is that it absolutizes its own version of the sacred. The Torah, Christ, and the Qur'an are each "the way" to their followers. They are each eternal, each the all-sufficient Tree of Life. It is part of the nature of religion to encourage absolute, centered, and sacred faithfulness to its own vehicles.[3] So great is the power and glory of Christ's resurrection, states a Russian Orthodox saying, that on Easter Sunday it is impossible to sin. Similar things are said by others of their own holy times. Every high-level religious guru in India is "the supreme Lord of the Universe." Every evangelical faith, whether Muslim, Christian, Jewish, Hindu, or Buddhist, is "the one, true faith." Such is the nature of religious discourse.

There is no need to argue about such vocabularies as though they were philosophical truth claims.[4] They are expressions of a relationship one has to the sacred. Faith is not an empirical proposition, but a relationship, like, "I will trust in you;" or a declaration of intent, like, "I will follow this path;" or a form of perception, like, "This is the way I see the truth."

Religious language not only particularizes and commits, but also universalizes and deepens itself. The insider's point of view can be not only defensive but generous, not only narrow but global, not only literalistic but mystical in its level of interpretation.

Do religions, being limited to their own visions, actually have theories of religion that in any way parallel what we have been describing in this book? Isn't a theory of religion exactly what they don't have, being religions themselves? In some ways the modern Western philosophers of religion[5] represent an impressive sequence of attempts to give rational meaning and justification to the subject, and were this to have been a longer survey, they would be given a section of their own. But our focus will be more on the religious than the philosophical context of viewing religion. There are several features of religious interpretation that illustrate our study of this kind of perspectival framing.

We will consider four ways in which religion interprets religion. After looking at (1) how historical religions are themselves products of interpretive activity, we review (2) ways religions interpret the diversity of religions; (3) ways religions deepen their understanding of religion through the idea of levels of meaning; and (4) ways religions link understanding with the religious capacity of the interpreter. Examples will be drawn from a spectrum of traditions.

The Formation of Religion through Interpretation

The major religions did not drop out of the blue, but arose as a result of interpretive innovations within their own histories. In this sense, the history of religion is itself the history of religious interpretations of religion. Consider some examples.

Judaism reconceived itself in a whole series of responses to historical changes. The shifts from tribal life to an established kingdom with a temple cult, and then to life in exile as a minority culture, were met with corresponding shifts in self-interpretation, including changed notions of piety. For example, when the Jerusalem temple, the "center of the world," was destroyed in 70 C.E., never to be rebuilt, more and more focus was placed on the exposition of scripture. Rabbis, exegetes of the Torah, replaced the former priesthood, administrators of sacrificial rites. The Torah in a sense became the sacred place, and elaborate, comprehensive Talmudic commentaries defined access to it. Judaism reinvented itself as a people of scriptural laws to be honored, rather than as a kingdom centered religiously around a temple cult.

Christianity, through Jesus and Saint Paul, began virtually as a reinterpretation of Judaism. In the Christian synoptic Gospels, Jesus is presented as the great interpreter of "the law and the prophets," creating a new religious emphasis on the life of the spirit rather than the letter of the law. In Saint Paul's letters, Christian faith is even more specifically construed as the successor to the previous Jewish religion of the law. Where before, Paul says, we lived as slaves to the Commandments, now we can live as heirs to God's grace through his Son. New Testament theology is scarcely intelligible outside the matrix of its intimate, interpretive connection to Judaism.

The formative periods of Jewish and Christian thought were grounded in exegesis of the scriptures and in the construction of its official interpretation over against the views of abundant unorthodox readings. One group of heretical exegetes, the Gnostics,[6] offered spiritualized allegorical renderings of the Bible—for example, construing the god of Genesis not as the supreme reality and not as the Father of Jesus, but as a jealous ruler of "this lower world" who had subjected Adam and Eve to his service. In such challenges the very nature of Christianity was at stake, and the challenges were met by counter-interpretations, often in the genre of formal creeds. When Protestantism emerged, it too defined itself against Catholicism as a truer, more faithful reading of scripture.

As with Christianity, so with Islam, which presented itself as a reformation of the Judeo-Christian tradition. Islam saw itself as the continuation, restoration, and final fulfillment of biblical faith, and like Christianity, it is not intelligible apart from the interpretive canopy by which it understands its linkage with preceding religious traditions.

The idea of progressive reinterpretation was to continue in virtually thousands of offshoots of the biblical tradition, each with a distinctive exegetical focus through which it saw itself as replacing previous dispensations. Baha'i, Mormonism, Christian Science, and the Unification Church are examples. Baha'i, formed in the nineteenth century, sees its founder Baha'u'llah as the last of the great prophets, who included Moses, Buddha, Jesus, and Muhammed. It features doctrines of the unity of religions and of all humanity, the equality of men and women, and the positive roles of science and political democracy—illustrative of how new religions bring together modern values and old roots into interpretive wholes.

Hinduism represents a three-thousand-year sequence of continuous self-reflection. Its scriptures, the Vedas (ca. 1000–400 B.C.E.), contain a sequence of evolving religious exegeses of previous religious concepts. For example, the final sections, the Upanishads, reinterpreted the rituals of the earlier sections so that all external acts were now to be understood as symbolic constructions of an inner, eternal self. Later Hinduism elaborated endlessly on ways of knowing this spiritual reality through various gods and yogas.

The history of Buddhism is one of developing interpretations of the concepts of Buddhahood and enlightenment. From these reconceptions came the many and radically different denominations of Tibet, China, and Japan. The new interpretations in essence came to function as new scriptures. While early Buddhism construed the Buddha as an extraordinary human who had achieved nirvana, later Buddhism came to understand the historical Buddha as a manifestation of the eternal Buddha, the great cosmic being that is the ultimate ground of all of us. Enlightenment, therefore, which in the earliest traditions is the goal to be attained after arduous self-perfection, is interpreted in some of the later Mahayana traditions as a reality we already possess but ordinarily fail to realize.

In such cases, a religion is not just something that *has* an interpretive tradition within it, but rather *is* an interpretive tradition.

Religion sometimes appears doctrinally unchanging, a fixed bulwark of creeds. But the activity known in biblical tradition as theology, and which has equivalents in other religions, is a constant process of creatively expositing the meaning of one's religion to the current generation. What does it mean *today* to be a Christian, Jew, or Buddhist? What does one's tradition have to say about questions of the environment, sexuality, poverty, evolution, politics, psychology, and secularization? What should God, salvation, ritual, morality, enlightenment, evil, scripture, or religious language mean in modern life? How should we think of other religions? And how can the faith be defended against the critics? It is interpretation that provides answers to these ongoing questions.

Religious Interpretations of Religious Diversity

From within religion has come a variety of explanations of the meaning of religious diversity. Religious positions range from the simplest forms of defensive, exclusivistic thinking, which identify the insider's religion as the only true one and all others as false, to various ideas about the partial validity of other religions, to concepts of universalism and pluralism which maintain the equality of all religions.

We have previously seen how the very concept of comparative religion changed through the centuries, and how the image and knowledge of other religions kept developing. The definition and significance of "other religions" will therefore vary depending on whether one is viewing them from Japan in the twelfth century, Palestine in the tenth century B.C.E., Rome in the first century C.E., or North America in the twenty-first century. Religions formed against the backdrop of the religious life in their own horizon. Biblical Judaism did not create itself in juxtaposition to Buddhism, but rather in relation to other Near Eastern traditions.

Varieties of Christian Interpretations. For the purpose of illustrating the diverse ways any one religion can view its coexistence with others, Christian examples will suffice.

The most traditional Christian writers had a whole repertoire of ways of interpreting nonbiblical religions—groups customarily lumped together by the designation "paganism."

One view focused on the idea of demonic origins. There were two variants here. The first was to maintain that pagan religions were the product of corrupted, fallen human minds and hearts, whose gods and rites could therefore be viewed as expressions of fear, lust, and ignorance. The second was to maintain that pagan gods were in reality demons, that is, it was really Satan who was seeking to be worshiped through them. Where missionaries encountered religions that seemed to include likenesses of Christian symbols or practices, they often interpreted this as the mocking, aping work of the Evil One.

In contrast to negative theories were those positing that all humans are made in the image of God, and thus that all humans have a capacity for basic knowledge about the divine. There is a "natural religion" available to all, though the special revelation of God through Christ is a gift that is not innate.

"Historical" explanations were also popular. One interpretive strategy was to show that paganism could be traced back to biblical times and influence, from which it had since become corrupted and fallen into polytheism. On the assumption that all cultures derived from the three sons of Noah—Ham, Shem, and Japheth—after the Flood, ingenious "histories" were produced to demonstrate a supposed geographic diffusion of images and practices. Sometimes theories of plagiarism were applied; for example, Greek temple designs were explained as having been copied from the temple blueprint originally given to Moses by God on Mount Sinai.

A variant explanation was that the pagan gods, like Zeus, had once been historical heroes and kings who were later elevated to divine status. The appeal of this interpretation was in showing that such supposed deities were not really gods at all.

Finally, symbolic or allegorical interpretations were also a common traditional tool. Here the gods and mythologies of others were construed as symbols or signs of Christian truths. Athena, for example, was said to represent God's wisdom. Christians had learned to do this by reading everything in the Hebrew scriptures as a prefiguration of Christ: Isaac carrying the wood for his own sacrifice was interpreted as a type or symbol of Jesus carrying the cross, the sacrificial Passover lamb was a symbol of the death of Christ, and Noah's ark was a symbol of the Church itself.

In more modern times, the interpretation of non-Christian religions has shown more concern with Asian religions and has largely abandoned the amorphous concept of paganism. Again, there is a range of options.

Perhaps the predominant modern Christian approach has been the attempt to demonstrate the superiority of Christian ideas to those of other religions. Typically this takes place by a certain stereotyping of positions. Biblical ideas that creation is "good" are made to look more attractive than oriental ideas that the world is an "illusion;" the idea of incarnate love is made to look more religiously profound by contrasting it with the idea of an "empty nirvana;" the idea that God is known through history and social justice can be made to look more adequate than the idea of "timeless" transcendental truths; and the idea that humans need to overcome their broken relationship to God can be made to look more realistic than the need for "simply realizing your inner potential." Such contrasts effectively set up the comparison not in the interests of objective comparative typologies, but in order to establish the supremacy of the interpreter's own faith by presenting others in terms of a belittling polarity.

Pluralism, on the other hand, has been more recently advocated by some as an option.[7] Here is the concept of respectful coexistence—that the many religions are valid but different ways of practicing religious life and of describing the one divine, indescribable reality. Agreement about doctrine is not necessary. It is possible for Christians to view Christ as absolute for themselves without drawing the negative conclusion that he is the one and only point of contact with God. "We can say that there is salvation in Christ without having to say that there is no salvation other than in Christ,"[8] writes the Christian theologian John Hick. The world faiths are varied but independently authentic contexts of salvation or liberation.

Often part of a pluralistic approach is the activity of creative dialogue between religions, where each stands to learn from the other and perhaps even to be changed in some ways by the other, in an atmosphere of complementarity.[9]

The approach of some Christian philosophies of religion has been to define the universal nature of religion and then in turn show how different religions represent different forms of that common function. Religiousness has thus been defined as "ultimate concern," or as the "experience of the numinous," with the corollary that Christianity is historically the most complete realization of these.[10]

Finally, there are transconceptual, spiritual, or experiential interpretations of religion that de-emphasize doctrine and all historical, outward differences, and which choose instead to think of religiousness as something that takes place at the level of spirit, removed from divisive concepts and philosophies.[11] Parallel to this approach is the view that all religions, including Christianity, are "man-made" relative to God's grace. Religious faith here is ultimately what God gives, not what humans do. Who would dare to define the boundaries of his activities? The Catholic Church affirmed that, apart from membership in the Church Visible, there are humans who follow the natural moral laws that God has written in every human heart, who live honorable lives, and who are therefore part of the Church Invisible. In a sense they are "anonymous Christians."[12]

While these are all Christian examples, similar interpretive stances are found in other religions. The idea of the uniqueness of one's own religion is not unique, nor are comparative demonstrations of the superiority of one's faith, nor is interpreting other religions as false, nor is pluralism, nor is the idea that religion is ultimately a matter of piety rather than doctrine. The Dalai Lama of Tibet, for example, preaches that love is the essence of all religion and cuts through all dogmatic differences.

Today non-Western religions are not just targets of Christian stereotypes, but active participants and challengers in the comparative process. The method of superior-inferior comparisons, for example, has worked not only for but against Christianity. Christianity thus has been categorized as male-oriented rather than holistic, bound rigidly to its own dualities rather than percipient of the overarching divine unity, externally rather than inwardly oriented with an impoverished rather than positive view of the inner self. Buddhists, on their end of the dialogue, claim that Christianity clings too much to its religious objects and fails to see that they are themselves symbols pointing to a deeper reality, a reality that transcends the distinction of self and god. Western religion, the criticism continues, needs to break through its idea of a self-contained ego and its reliance on an objectified, externalized god. [13]

Varieties of Universalism. Alongside the viewpoints of particular religions is one that can be labeled "universalism." It, too, is an inside standpoint. It is the view that all religions essentially point toward the same reality but use different names for it. As water is the same everywhere, but is called by different names, so too with divinity or the spirit that is in everything. All religions affirm a supreme reality to which we are in some way accountable. But each has its own terms for this reality. Universalism, sometimes called "the perennial philosophy," [14] has had exponents in many times and places, in many religions, and has not always been connected with organized religion.

Universalism has had various Western versions. The idea that humans are part of a timeless spectrum embracing physicality at one extreme, reason in the middle, and soul or spirit at the other is a concept that goes back to Plato. In the seventeenth and eighteenth centuries, universalism was sometimes illustrated in Deism, which, as we have seen, maintained the idea of a supreme God while denying the validity of specific supernatural claims. Deists distinguished between lower and higher religion—the former being the superstitions, anthropomorphisms, and ethnic loyalties of the masses, and the latter being the nobler insights into the enduring, universal religious truths of the world. Many in the Western tradition have looked for and believed they have found distilled, common truths in the world's religions, e.g., the affirmation of a spiritual order and the necessity of a corresponding moral integrity on the part of humans.

Yet the most influential modern type of universalism came into Western thought through Asian philosophies. Here the religious unity of the world is seen in somewhat more mystical terms, terms that are usually perceived as a corrective to biblical narrowness. Cosmic perspective here replaces historical and nationalistic perspectives. Experience replaces dogma. Inner unity with God replaces Christian devaluations of human beings as sinners. There is one supreme reality of which we are all expressions, and this reality can be realized within through any number of spiritual disciplines.

Hindu scriptures themselves contain the seeds of universalistic thinking, just as the Bible contains many ideas about the uniqueness of revelation that are antithetical to universalism. The central theme of classical Hindu thought is that there is one supreme reality, Brahman, that is beyond any naming or form. Just as "You shall have no other gods before Me," is representative of early biblical religious outlooks, so "Truth is One, the sages say, but people call it by many names," is a favorite universalist quote from the oldest strata of the Indian heritage, the Rig Veda. In Hinduism hundreds of names for God coexist, and all the gods are construed as the masks of the supreme God. In addition, Hinduism teaches about a variety of paths to divine realization, accepting the idea that people will be of different temperaments and stations in life, and will therefore need different kinds of disciplines.

All religions, in this fashion, are seen simply as different symbolisms for the same ultimate reality. When modern Hindus articulated their views about biblical religions it was natural for them, with this overarching concept of spirituality, to accept that Jesus was an incarnation of God, though one among many. Hindus have traditionally believed in a plurality of special incarnations of God, not inconsistent with their view that God is ultimately in everything. It was also natural for them to maintain that one could come to God through any spiritual teacher or symbol, and that there was no need to change one's given paths to God. The best known nineteenth-century saint, Sri Rama-krishna, tried finding God through several religious paths, including devotion to Christ and the Muslim Allah, and claimed to have arrived at the same goal through each.

To universalists, other religious traditions also seemed to include versions of this generous outlook. Certainly Buddhism and Taoism supplied religious models for universalism, with the concept that there is a ubiquitous supreme reality—a Buddha nature or Tao—that is beyond linguistic definition. Buddhists also accept that there are great saints (bodhisattvas) in the world who will use whatever means are necessary to help people become free from their ignorance and suffering, so that it would be consistent to believe "that Buddhas appear also in the guise of teachers of other religions for those beings for whom such religions are appropriate."[15] Buddhists can easily see Jesus as a bodhisattva. Finally, the mystical literature of the West also has been a resource for universalism. Read from an Asian point of view, the lives and teachings of saints and mystics East and West illustrate the global commonality of spiritual experience.

Reading the World: Levels of Religious Meaning

To learn a religion is to learn how it interprets its texts, including the great "text," the world itself.

Different religions focus their readings on different areas and kinds of experience. Tribal and archaic religion reads nature as though it were scripture. Diviners read the signs of the gods in the patterns of the elements—the flight of birds, the lines of an animal liver, the images of a dream, the outbreak of an illness. So obvious is it that everything is a manifestation of spirit, that often interpreters put themselves at the disposal of the spirit world through trance.

On the other hand, religions based on scripture read their texts as carefully and intensively as others read nature, seeking to grasp the purposes of God or to fathom the messages of the Buddhas. In either case, religion scans its worlds to uncover what is not seen by the ordinary eye. Philosophers of religion do this, but so do shamans in states of trance. Even religions based on meditation and introspection teach adherents to read diligently the activities of their own minds and behavior, day in and day out, in order to arrive at a more profound self-understanding.

The very act of interpreting in religious terms an otherwise nonreligious situation or event—for example construing one's suffering in terms of Christ's suffering, or viewing obstacles as opportunities to become more enlightened—shows the creative, life-effecting side of interpretation. In these cases the power of interpretation itself rearranges or transfigures one's world. Much of the power and efficacy of religious piety and belief is found in the magic of such lens adjustments.

The distinctive nature of religious meaning is not simply that one thing is seen to represent another conceptually. Meaning is

not just denotative, as a red light stands for "stop," or the image of
a lily stands for purity. Much more specific to religion than cognitive representation is the participatory character of meanings and
symbols. Religious symbols and words do not simply signify, they
speak and perform—and in doing so they transform perception,
punctuate the routine world with their own power, effect felt
presences, and engage the participant. The purpose of religious
language is not just to represent a world but to act one out. The
sacred is enacted through words, stories, images, and the construction of consecrated space and time.

When the Sioux Indians build a sweat lodge, it is not just a
collection of branches and rocks that represent certain cosmic
ideas, but an enactment of those ideas. To enter the lodge's
darkness and reemerge purified into the light is to recreate life, not
just to describe it. When the rabbis maintain that even the
number of bones in the human body (613) corresponds by divine
synchronicity to the number of laws of Moses, we understand that
this is neither an anatomical nor mathematical meaning, but a
religious affirmation of the immanence of God's rule in the very
structure, the very bones, of creation.

Thus the act of interpretation ultimately derives from acts of
piety. As we see God to be, so we will interpret.

In mystical interpretations of the world, all that might otherwise seem ordinary becomes extraordinary. The Hindu Upanishads speak of the divine Self looking out through the eyes of
everything—the old man with a stick, the young girl, the green
parrot. In Shingon Buddhism each thing in the universe is an
"expressive symbol" (*monji*) of the body of the supreme Buddha.
We are all part of the mental, verbal, and bodily activity of
Buddha's enlightenment, the so-called three mysteries, and
through enlightened practice in the ordinary world we can become aware of how everyday things and events are intimations of
Buddha's own process. In mystical forms of Russian Christianity,
monks practice seeing Christ in every human face. "All things,"
the Gospel of John reads, "were made through Him." In the
central act of ritual Christianity, the Eucharist, the consecrated
bread *is* the actual body of Christ, not merely a symbol of it.
Again, religious interpretation is not just theory but observance.

Interpreting Scripture. In many religions, interpretation means
scriptural interpretation. Lifetimes are spent fathoming the sacred
meanings of these words.

But scriptures *are* scriptures only through the screens of interpretation. They do not come interpreted, but must *be* interpreted. Christians interpret everything in the Hebrew Old Testament as a preparation for the coming of Christ. Even in the New Testament, Catholics and Protestants will explain the same phrase differently in conformity with their respective doctrinal universes. Thus when Jesus says, "You are Peter, and on this rock I will build my church," Catholics read the rock as the inauguration of the institution of the papacy (Peter being the first Pope), but Protestants read the rock to be Peter's expression of faith in Jesus, faith having a primacy in Protestantism comparable to the Church in Catholicism.

What anything in the Bible is "about" will be a result of the terms in which it is read.[16] Is the Garden of Eden story to be read as a sexist message about the subordination of women, expressing the demotion of Eve from her original status as a goddess, or as a conventional parable of disobedience? Is it a mystical allegory of the fall of consciousness into the separate world of opposites, or is it a literal account of real events that happened at a real time and place? Is the serpent good for bringing about self-consciousness, or evil for bringing about sin? The words of the Bible can be read to support any philosophy or theology, just as they have been read to support every conceivable social practice, including slavery, polygamy, holy war, nationalism, capitalism, and witch burning.

To take the case of the Hebrew Torah, rabbinic tradition believes that the legacy of interpreting it began at Mount Sinai, at the same time the written tradition of Moses was given. The oral tradition of commentaries is thus the critical means of bringing forth the real meaning of the written text. One therefore does not simply study the Torah alone, but through the Talmud—which brings together the fruits of the oral tradition and which contains the classic exegetical guidelines for interpreting scripture. The Talmud is the prescriptive lens through which the meaning of the Torah is seen, mediating much of the literalness of the text and enlarging on its spiritual meanings. The value of the oral Torah is shown in a commentary that compares God to a king who gave his two servants each a measure of wheat and a bundle of flax: "While the foolish servant did nothing at all with the wheat and flax, the wise servant baked bread from the wheat and spun a cloth from the flax. 'Now when the Holy One, blessed be He, gave the Torah to Israel, he gave it to them only in the form of wheat, to extract from it fine flour, and flax, to extract from it a garment.' "[17]

Because the scripture is the inexhaustible "word of God," its interpretation will be inexhaustible. There can be no end to fathoming its meanings. Commentators find meaning in every syllable. One of the great students of Torah stated that his work was but a drop from the ocean of knowledge: "If all the seas were ink, and the reeds pens, and the heaven and earth scrolls, and all humankind scribes, they would not be sufficient to write the Torah that I have learned, and I have taken from it no more than a man would take by dipping the point of his pen into the sea."[18]

Rabbinic commentary, particularly in the mystical traditions of the Kabbala, supplied other metaphors of the interpretive layers of the Torah. The Torah is likened to a nut with a hard outer shell, finer inner coverings, and a kernel. The medieval *Zohar* compares the process of coming to knowledge of the Torah to the process of a lover gaining gradual access to a palace in which a beautiful woman (the Torah) beckons. As he progresses, by occasional glimpses and signals of her in the window, through the gates of outer meanings to the inner chambers (i.e., of meaning), he finally becomes "the bridegroom of the Torah," is with her face to face, and she can "converse with him concerning all of her secret mysteries, and all the secret ways which have been hidden in her heart from immemorial time."[19] The more the interpreter understands, the more the Torah reveals. And then there is the "outer clothing" simile:

> For when the angels descend to earth they don earthly garments, else they could neither abide in the world, nor could it bear to have them. But if this is so with the angels, then how much more so it must be with the Torah: the Torah it was that created the angels and created all the worlds and through Torah are all sustained. The world could not endure the Torah if she had not garbed herself in garments of this world.
>
> Thus the tales related in the Torah are simply her outer garments, and woe to the man who regards that outer garb as the Torah itself, for such a man will be deprived of portion in the next world.[20]

"Just as wine must be kept in a jar," the commentary continues, "so the Torah must be contained in an outer garment."[21]

Similar interpretations have been made of all scriptures and objects that focalize the sacred.

The concept of multiple levels of meaning in scripture was crucial in Judeo-Christian theology from its beginning.[22] Among other reasons, this was done to show Greco-Roman audiences that the Bible was a work of depth comparable to philosophies like Platonism. The violent battles of the Old Testament could then be seen on a higher plane, pointing to the warfare of Christians against the hosts of wickedness in heavenly places. The Jordan River could be understood as the river of death that one must ultimately cross; the temple at Jerusalem symbolizes the heavenly city as Eden does paradise; and the food laws of Moses could be given the moral meaning of referring not just to mere abstention from the flesh of certain animals, but from the vices imaginatively associated with the animals. Everything in the Bible was here symbolic of spiritual meanings, and deciphering the figurative senses unfolded the divine intention. By medieval times, the idea of the fourfold literal, moral, allegorical, and mystical levels of scriptural interpretation was taken for granted.

Transcending Language. One strand of religious interpretation tries to push beyond words and language altogether, for the purpose of acknowledging that the true object of religion cannot be completely dealt with by any concepts. Traditions in Taoism and Zen Buddhism exemplify this well. The opening lines of the Chinese classic, the *Tao Te Ching,* are that "The Tao that is spoken of is not the absolute Tao." Zen speaks of a transmission of interpretation *outside* scriptures, a lineage not of principles but of direct experience of the truth of enlightenment. This line of transmission traces itself to a sermon the Buddha gave in which he said nothing, but only held up a flower. Only Mahakasyapa, the first of the line of Zen teachers, understood. In training regimens, monks are given riddles (*koans*) to ponder and then interpret to their teachers. These questions (for instance, "What is the sound of one hand clapping?") require the mind to overcome its own false dichotomizings and dependencies on the objectifying nature of language.

Religious interpretation here is linked with the deconstructive act of overcoming illusory grids of meanings.[23] It is not something solemnly added on or embellished, but an act of *dis*illusioning, *de*objectifying, and *dis*mantling—an act of freedom. It is a swat on the back, a laugh, or a scream—all to jostle the mind out of its linguistic prison and into the open air of Buddha nature. Some meditation techniques therefore emphasize the process of stepping back from the flow of mental life and observing the projection-making activity of the mind—providing an interesting solution, within Buddhist terms, to the challenge of Freudian critiques that religion is but a projective device.

Levels of Religious Understanding

The idea that the Torah discloses herself to those who love her draws attention to the religious capacities of the human interpreter. According to many religious traditions, there are those who see only the outer garments of religion, and those who see its soul. The religious object—the scripture, the Buddha, God— reveals itself in correlation with a religious *act* of perception on our part. As *we* are, religiously, so are the gods, so are the scriptures, and so is the world. This relationship needs to be looked at more closely.

Jewish tradition held that the revelation at Mount Sinai "was heard by each individual Israelite according to his/her own strength and level of consciousness."[24]

> The sixteenth-century Kabbalists of Safed, elaborating on this conception, developed the idea that there are 600,000 aspects or modes of expounding the Torah, which correspond to the 600,000 souls who are traditionally said to have been present at Mount Sinai and who, according to the laws of transmigration, are present in every generation of Israel. Moses Cordovero of Safed (d. 1570 C.E.) proclaimed that each of these 600,000 primordial souls has its own special portion of the Torah, "and to none other than he, whose soul springs from thence, will it be given to understand it in this special and individual way that is reserved to him."[25]

Like the Buddha's teaching, the Torah appears and is interpreted differently in each "world"—in this case the earthly world, the world of angels, and the higher light world.

Religions typically observe that spirituality is relative to stages of knowledge. Sometimes this means initiatory knowledge, as members are inducted into the mysteries of the group's rites and mythologies. The case of the French ethnographer Marcel Griaule has come to stand for something of a minor revolution in anthropological attitudes about primitives. After Griaule had studied the African Dogon tribe for several years, an elder finally inducted him into the "real" spiritual knowledge of their religious system. Thenceforth Griaule understood what he had missed and had not known before. He was shown the living correspondences

between everyday objects—like the tribe's working granaries—
and cosmic, divine realities. He had discovered the hidden Dogon
metaphysic. It turned out that during the first ten years of Griaule's fieldwork, his questions had all been answered "at a level of
instruction offered by elders to beginners,"[26] but that after he had
proved his good faith, a decision was made by the elders to instruct
him in the highest form of initiatory knowledge. Instead of the
natives being simply informants providing information that the
anthropologists then would compile into a knowledge about the
tribe, they have here reversed the roles and become the initiators
of the outside observers.

Each religious system has its own understanding of such
stages. In the West, Platonic philosophy distinguished levels of
knowledge leading from sensory perception up through mental
conceptions and on to the ecstatic, direct vision of the divine.
This format of a "ladder of knowing" was to have a deep influence
on Christian mysticism, which developed notions of various and
complex stages of purification of the soul. In devotional Hinduism, where the love of God is the primary concept of religious
life, one finds highly defined successive stages of relationships to
the divine, such as acquaintance, friend, and lover. In systems
where doctrine is important, training in levels of argumentation
brings one through levels of mastery and knowledge. Within each
religion there are stages of comprehension and hierarchies of
knowing.

Levels of Enlightenment: Buddhist Examples. Buddhism shows some
of the best examples of how the interpretation of religion is
connected with the capacity of the religious participants.

The later, or Mahayana, Buddhists found that they needed to
account for what appeared to be doctrinal discrepancies between
previous schools of Buddhism. They developed the concept that
the Buddha had taught at different levels according to the capacity of understanding of his followers. He had employed expedient
or "skillful means" (*upaya*) to determine what various followers
needed to hear and were able to hear. Just as a physician dispenses
varying treatments according to different ailments, so the Buddha
in his wisdom spoke to a spectrum of human needs. The Buddhist
philosopher Nagarjuna thus wrote:

> Just as a grammarian [first] makes
> His students read the alphabet,

So the Buddha taught his disciples
The doctrines they could forbear.

To some he taught doctrines
To turn away from wickedness;
To some, doctrines for acquiring merit;
To others, doctrines based on duality.

To some he taught doctrines based on non-duality; to some
He taught what is profound and frightening to the timid,
Having an essence of emptiness and compassion,
The method for achieving enlightenment.[27]

Buddhists created many versions of the plural stations of religious understanding. One is even in the form of a colossal, nine-terraced stone pyramid at Borobudur, Java, where each level represents a different stage of Buddhist teaching and understanding. Pilgrims recapitulate these in a journey to the summit. The Shingon school of Buddhism, for its part, worked out a ten-stage classification of religious teachings based on as many steps of the path of enlightenment.[28] The hierarchy corresponded to schools of religion that were extant in ninth-century Japan. The rankings were:

1. The Deluded, Ramlike State of Mind
2. The Ignorant, Childlike, but Tempered State of Mind
3. The Infantlike, Composed State of Mind
4. The State of Mind Recognizing Only Mental Behavior, Not Self, as Real
5. The State of Mind Free of Karmic Seeds
6. The Mahayana State of Mind Concerned with Others
7. The State of Mind Awakened to the Unborn Nature of Mind
8. The State of Mind Following the One Path without Artifice
9. The State of Mind Completely without Individuated Essence
10. The State of Mind Esoteric and Glorious

Briefly, the first level is a nonreligious, subhuman state devoid of any moral regulation. The second type, represented by the Confucianists, recognizes the need for morality, but cannot understand life beyond the values of social harmony. The third type (Taoists) see the possibility of something more to life than the social, but their version of transcendence is dreamy and childlike.

The fourth and fifth types (Theravadin Buddhists) see the universality of impermanence and overcome the idea of an immortal self, but they are still individualistic in trying to find enlightenment just for themselves.

The sixth through ninth stages rank versions of Mahayana teachings. All are universalistic. Each emphasizes a particular form of the unity of transcendence and immanence (i.e., unity of wisdom and compassion; unity of nirvana and world; oneness of paths to enlightenment; and the interpenetration of all things.) But the tenth level, through special esoteric practice, generates direct, intimate participation in Buddhahood. It is experiential and not just philosophical, and is the ultimate way of Shingon Buddhism.

Finally, Zen Buddhism presents an example of religious progress in the famous series of "ox-herding pictures."[29] A set of ten drawings shows the sequence of stages of enlightenment, where the man represents consciousness and the ox represents Buddha or his teachings. Thus the first pictures show the man in confusion, with no sign of the ox at all, followed by his sightings of the ox, his joining up with the ox, his reliance on the ox, and his gradual mastery of the ox. But in the later pictures the ox disappears, since there comes a point on the spiritual path where one no longer needs to rely on outward religious objects; and then there is an empty circle where the man too has disappeared—indicating that one has here become free from all sense of a separate self. The penultimate picture shows a scene from nature, indicating that the mind is now transparent to the Buddhahood of the larger world (there is no more subject-object division, no more man versus ox). Finally there is an image of the man now back amidst the townsfolk, returning to the world as a giver and transformer of others.

Spiritual Evolutionism: East-West Syntheses. Some modern religious philosophies have correlated worldviews with developmental stages of the evolution of consciousness. One of these "transpersonal psychology" viewpoints, which draws both on psychological ego theory and Asian concepts of enlightenment, will serve as an example.[30] Here eight levels of awareness are distinguished, each with a correspondingly different worldview.

(1) Archaic, (2) magical, and (3) mythic worldviews correspond here to as many stages of pre-egoic development. The first

identifies self with everything around it; its surroundings are more or less parts of the self's own body. It is a stage of nondifferentiation. In the second phase, "self and physical world are just barely differentiated," remaining "magically involved" with each other. It is a stage of narcissistic grandiosity, of manipulation. The third, mythic stage continues the differentiation. The self no longer thinks it can order the world around, but "transfers that magical belief to real or imaginary figures in the environment, the figures of myth." Its outlook is, "I can no longer move the world, but God can." Myth and belief are here concretistic and fundamentalistic.

A subsequent stage is that of rationality, marking a divide between prerational and postrational religious experience. Following the rational stage is the existential one, a kind of "higher" mental ability that allows one to begin unifying the different parts of one's existence. The existentialist writers (e.g., Kierkegaard, Nietzsche, Buber, Tillich, Jaspers, and Rollo May) have addressed this moment of self-accountability.

On the other side of rationality and existentialism are three mystical stages. The psychic stage is the first in which one experiences a liberating, higher spiritual nature, e.g., in nature or the surroundings. The seventh stage is represented by the saint—the understanding that "there is a spiritual dimension above or beyond mere nature, or what you can see with your physical senses." This is "God-mysticism." But there is still some dualistic difference between soul and God here. Finally, the last stage is that of pure nondualism, the realm of the sage. The sage is the point where the self has transcended separateness altogether. It is the final paradigm shift.

The Reciprocity Principle. Much religious teaching, especially at the level of practice, appears to be about such paradigm shifts—shifts not just in how we picture objects but in how we relate to objects. The world of the sacred shows itself reciprocally with the states of mind of its participants.

This reciprocity is expressed in biblical maxims like "seek and ye shall find," or "he who believes in me will have eternal life," or Asian observations like "the ignorant see only the world, but the wise see God," or "Truth waits for eyes unclouded by longing." Religious "reality"—whether conceived as God or as an inner self—becomes in religious terms a function of such transactions. The mystic Meister Eckhart said that "the eye wherein I see God is the same eye wherein God sees me."[31] Perhaps this is the religious version of "the scale creates the phenomenon."

Thus in the frame of religious interpretation, human consciousness is explicitly part of the frame. Only like knows like. The appearance of the sacred relates to the transformations of the religious participant's own subjectivity. We human beings are part of the reality equation.

The participant's situation is a variable in several ways. One is the requirement of religious fitness for communication with the sacred. Initiation rites or various other forms of purification can serve this function. One must be in an appropriate receiving mode. Plains Indian vision quests required extensive fasting and other forms of deprivation in order to invite contact with guardian spirits. An Asian saying is that "when you are ready, and not a minute before or after, your guru appears," and evangelical theology says that unless you die to your old self and are reborn you cannot receive Christ and the kingdom of God. Spiritual directors advise aspirants about the obstructions of pride, and about the paradoxical variables of effort and effortlessness in arriving at one's goals and becoming transformed. "The adventure the hero is ready for," writes a comparative mythology scholar, "is the one he gets."[32]

Reflections on the Inside Religious Frame

The insider's religious voice is part of the lives of millions—many more than those who try to explain religion from the outside. It is a worldwide form of discourse, and varies in content as world horizons change. Contrary to some predictions, it does not appear to be going away.

For rationalists, of course, the main issue about religious views is their truth. How, it is asked, can their claims be verified? Are the gods really there independent of our frames? Do religions refer to realities that are agencies in their own right?

The questions are natural, yet the dilemma is that they presuppose a space in which they can be objectively or neutrally answered. But is there any? There does not seem to be such a mediating arena or world unconnected to someone's assumptions about it, where the matter could be evidentially determined. Religious truths cannot be substantiated in any other framework than their own, though many philosophers have laboriously tried to create arguments for or against their objective validity. The religious paradigm posits its own data, terms, rules, and realities. Religious interpretation not only belongs within its own system— it is its own self-creating system.

The objects of religion, like God or Buddhahood, are only "known" in the context of religious acts. We have noticed that religious interpretation is not just something disembodied and ghostly, floating in the air, but is something that people *do*. All of the religious views described above illustrate the concept that linguistic world-building, that is, religious interpretation, is itself an activity rather than a subjectless theory. It is the activity of seeing the world as sacred, rather than seeing the world as social forces or as physical substances. The gods are not known independently of this active, experiential matrix. Without a religious subject, no religious objects, no religious data, come into view.

The concept of multiple data-creating frames and paradigms therefore means that we are no longer forced to choose between the objectivist, rationalist options that either the god exists or the god is an illusion—a dichotomy that has pervaded popular opinion just as much as it has philosophy and theology. Gods are ways of seeing the world, and these ways exist.

Everyone knows today that in an age of critical thinking, religious language cannot be taken for granted. But by the same token, neither can any other languages or ideologies that claim to describe exclusively *the* foundation of things.

By their nature, many religious systems are not built to produce theories of religion in general or make accurate representations of religions other than their own. They are designed for the practice and explanation of the sacred as they understand it within their tradition. To be an insider to anything is to have blind spots and a certain defensiveness about one's truths. It is to reduce reality to those truths.

The idea of a common reality that all religions point to is also not easy to defend, given the differences in religious worldviews. If one wishes to affirm that all religions are directed to the same religious reality, then it seems necessary to deny all those claims of particular religions that seem to picture reality differently than in universalistic terms. Some argue that this would not leave the religions in any recognizable form.[33] But whether or not the sameness can be justified on objective grounds, it is at least intelligible as a *religious* affirmation or belief in its own right, which is the context in which we have viewed universalism here. If one chooses to see all religions as engaged with the same reality, that is one's incontrovertible perceptual privilege.

Religious interpretation is not just a rigid, scholastic exercise, but can be creative and ingenious. In an instant, by an act of language, it transfigures matter into spirit, lead into gold. It can rearticulate the world, putting it in the light of every conceivable imagery and staging. It can even self-destruct, à la Zen. If critics of religion see religion as merely camouflaged psychological needs, religion can easily see psychological needs as camouflaged religious needs.

Finally, we have considered how reciprocity works within a religious frame. If we can say, "as society, so the gods," or "as the psyche, so the gods," then religion itself says, "as religiousness, so the gods." In a mirror effect, and with multiple kinds of cultural mirrors, religion reveals itself once again according to the way it is approached.

7

The Contextuality of Interpretation

We have tried to understand different interpretive frames through a clarification of the particular point of view from which each takes its rationale. While a number of pluralistic images have been used throughout this study—worlds, locations, lenses, standpoints, matrices, and languages—it is time now directly to focus and expand upon a factor which is at the basis of this variety and gives it intelligibility: context. Every interpretation is contextual, and understanding contextuality is the ultimate, clarifying step that illumines the nature and scope of interpretive frames.

The context of something is the interrelated network of conditions in which it exists. The term even has the root meaning of "woven together" (*com*, "together, with" + *texere*, "to weave"). The context of what someone says about religion is usually a tacit, hidden web of surrounding assumptions. In a sense, context is what is not said, yet is implied.

In practice we typically ignore this silent grounding because we are so preoccupied with the face value of what is being said or represented in an interpretation. We are naturally less interested in understanding the rationale of the interpretation than in agreeing or disagreeing with it. All the more reason, then, to analyze this factor of situatedness closely and respectfully.

We will first consider examples of the multiple character of location and standpoint, and then go on to show how this root concept of perspective leads, in its fuller implication, to the more rounded notion of context.

Images of Multiple Perspective

There are several ways to illustrate and metaphorize the perspectival, contextualist model.

Places and Views. At the basis of the concept of context is the element of place. Place creates context: It is context in its bedrock form. Place includes not just geographic but also conceptual location. It is shaped by ideological and religious canopies of meaning, cultural value-orientations, rules governing social protocols, regional settings and points in space, moments in time and history, biographic factors, immediate circles of conversation, and current circumstances. It is around place, made up of factors like these, that a world rises up.

Interpretation is never disembodied. When we see the world and when we see religion we always do so from somewhere. They look different according to where one is standing, as a cone-shaped object will appear different from the bottom, from the top, and from the side. Visually, it will not be the same object. The angles seem to give contradictory data.

Any object is subject to such aspectual, selective vision. A stream seen from the air may appear as part of a wide pattern of other streams and landscape designs, but to someone fishing in the middle of it, the water presents itself in quite another, participatory mode. We can see things as parts of patterns or we can see them singly; we can see things from detached observation points or as actors within them.

Religion is like any visual object where only one side at a time can be viewed, and the life and variety of its interpretation stems from this insinuative fact. There has formed a landscape of interpretation corresponding to the landscape of religious life. Those parts of religion that are visible to the interpreter's interested eye become the basis of interpretation. Not all religion is of concern, and about most of it, as about most parts of the world, we are both oblivious and ignorant. The place of the interpreter has determined where religion itself takes place.

Religion indeed has a complexity that is like the complexity of place. It has its shady parts of town and its palaces, its dead-end alleys and its broad highways, its private rendezvous spots and its central public squares, its settled, residential areas and its business districts (sometimes corrupt), its entertainment zones and its gang warfare turfs, its parks and its schools. If religion is literally all over the place, it is not surprising that interpretation will be, too.

Maps of the same city differ radically according to the angle of the subject matter mapped. Picturing any area quite differently would be the charts of the water department, the tourist bureau, political party organizations, cocaine dealers, and church parishes. Again, maps chart only material that is useful and relevant for the purposes of their makers, and ignore all other information as extraneous. Interpretations of religion are like such overlapping, mapped systems existing within the same town. Each makes sense given the selective nature of its data. Each "says" only what it is interested in.

In the great series of prints known as *Thirty-Six Views of Mount Fuji*, the Japanese artist Hokusai places the observer in stunningly different settings. These places are not just so many versions of the same view of the mountain, as with Monet's series paintings of haystacks and cathedrals which depict those objects according to the changing atmosphere and light of different times. To Hokusai, Mount Fuji appears *through* locations as discrepant as a teahouse party, a workplace scene with men on ladders, travelers on a road, boatmen at sea, and the circle of a large barrel that is in process of construction by a diffident cooper. The overwhelming impression is not the beauty or even richness of the mountain— and certainly not the conjuring of a neutral, postcard-type view of it as a look-at-me object—but the conspicuous, inevitably self-contained life of the subworlds in which Mount Fuji (or religion, in our case) then finds its multiple roles.

Likewise, James Joyce's classic novel *Ulysses*, which recapitulates the journey of Odysseus in terms of a day in the life of a Dubliner, takes us through the points of view of diverse characters in diverse settings within the city. With virtuosity we are led through the "standpoints" of libraries and bedrooms, bars and beach strands, all with their concomitant linguistic worlds and styles. Joyce portrays the simultaneity of these worlds with delicious artistry and irony and in several cases has them either encounter each other or silently and unknowingly crisscross.

Odysseus's journey becomes a modern voyage through the multiplicity of place and language.

If place is a metaphor which incorporates the important distinction of inside and outside, then landscape, city, and mountain are not just a series of objects to be noted by observers, but a series of habitations from which insiders look out. The above chapters have shown in several ways that religion is not just an object to look at, but also a subject that is itself the looker.

Timing. Complementing the notion of the plurality of place is that of timing and function. Interpretation is not only locational but circumstantial.

As hammers, screwdrivers, and saws all perform different yet noncompetitive functions, and as a tool that is right for one occasion may be wrong for another, each interpretive frame can be seen as a serviceable instrument, or as fit for performing a specific job. Like a tool, an idea or explanation that does something in one area may be useless in another. A particular key opens a particular door and not others, for which one needs other keys.

In the same way, we may find ourselves in revolving moments of interpretive need with regard to religion, depending on just what it is that requires clarification. The issue at hand may require explanation that is historical, or sociological, or psychological, or comparative. For psychological understanding we would not use sociological analysis, and vice versa. The issue may be local, inviting regional research, or it may be global, requiring cross-cultural analysis. Sometimes we need to pay strict attention to evidence and counterevidence, and sometimes we are called upon for imaginative reconstructions. Sometimes we are in a purely detached, scientific setting, and at other times we are in settings where moral judgment is appropriate or unavoidable. The wisdom of Ecclesiastes that "for everything there is a time and a season," surely applies also to the pivoting succession of interpretive circumstances.

Because interpretation is language, it contains, like a toolbox, functions appropriate to many different tasks.[1] It pins down but also expresses and poeticizes. It holds at a distance but also embodies and testifies. It is institutional but also casual. It is rhetorical and public but also intimately one-on-one. It is obligatory, pedantic, and servile; and it is audacious, stimulating, and playful. It is resonant with every conceivable mood and innuendo. Always performed through language, interpretive behavior embraces all the things humans do as speaking beings.

The plurality of interpretation therefore corresponds at least partly to the plurality of modes of language, which are in turn appropriate to shifting questions, settings, and audiences.

Multiple Meanings. Religious action can signify different things all at once, just as any act can be said to have multiple meanings or multiple causes.

What does it mean that Mr. Jones goes to church on Sunday? He may be doing so to (1) worship what he conceives to be the supreme being, (2) maintain a family tradition, (3) meet friends and socialize at the coffee hour afterwards, (4) get out of the house for a change of pace, (5) show off his suits, (6) relieve guilt, (7) avoid feeling guilty were he not to go, (8) give expression to his musical nature by singing in the choir, or (9) enjoy the experience of being part of a large supportive group. And so on.

Jones's act of church attendance may well connect with all these factors. They do not necessarily contradict each other, and could conceivably dovetail. Any religious act, as Eliade stressed, is simultaneously a social, psychological, and even biological act, because humans are layered beings whose lives take place in several intersecting matrices. Part of the force of religious symbols and acts is their capacity to satisfy many levels of meaning.

Mr. Jones is a multiplex being. He conceives of himself as a religious person, but also as a social person and a musical person. He is also unconscious of many of the ways his actions function to satisfy the various needs and desires of his life. Because Mr. Jones is complex, every act of his is complex. He lives in several matrices of meaning, both simultaneously and consecutively. Within each of these contexts going to church means something different. One could even say that at the most physical level, the reason Mr. Jones goes to church is because his body moves itself from one place to another. (That things have immediate, physical, material causes as well as ulterior causes is a concept that goes back at least to Aristotle.) Whatever surface reasons or rationalizations we may give for it, religious behavior can also function to satisfy and maintain any number of psychological and social needs.

The extent to which coexisting interpretations may or may not conflict will be taken up in the last chapter.

The Contextual Nature of Interpretation

The perspectival and complex nature of human situatedness means that the embracive notion of context now deserves fuller attention.

Three highly contextualized factors conjoin in the moment of interpretation: (1) the interpreter, (2) the interpreter's audience, and (3) the assumed object of interpretation. These will be analyzed separately to bring out the contributing function of each.

The Situation of the Interpreter. The interpreter of religion participates in the same variables of situatedness as the religious people he or she interprets. It is not just religion that is sociologically, psychologically, historically, and religiously varied; but also the one who interprets religion. We need to understand the settings and purposes of interpreters of religion just as we need to understand those of religious people. An interpreter always speaks or writes within the premises of a cultural and linguistic tradition. He or she configures religion through the specific issues and options of that tradition or subtradition, correcting previous views or adding to a sequence and milieu of related ideas. If we do not see what questions interpreters are responding to, if we do not see the "family" of dialogue in which they stand, we will hardly appreciate the solutions.

Sometimes the interpreter simply represents an institution or school of thought. Here the operative context is not personal or biographic factors, but the linguistic conventions or genres of the institutions. While we sometimes think of interpretation as the function of individual imagination, in historical cultures it is typically a matter of training—and even a bulwark of institutional authority. Primarily something to be learned and inculcated, it was typically not free form, but followed guidelines of doctrinal acceptability within a community. One was expected to spend a lifetime mastering commentaries on texts like the Confucian Classics or the Hindu Vedas, according to the doctrines of one's school.

Sometimes public law—whether religious or secular—determines what something official "means." If a fourteen-year-old joins a new religious sect and leaves home to undergo an intensive reeducation program, is this freedom of religious choice or is it kidnapping? The court decides. Is a Christmas tree in front of a town hall a religious symbol, or is it a secular, folk tradition and hence not a violation of church-state separation? Would adding some reindeer figures make it non-religious? Interpreting what is religious, whether at tribal or large-scale levels, whether identifying authors to be destroyed for blasphemy or foods permissible to eat, has historically often been relegated to official bodies.

At the same time, interpreting from noninstitutional positions often brings biographical contexts into play. The independently worked-out views of Freud and Jung pictured religion differently largely because of differences in the men's own life histories. Individual opinions about religion inevitably link with biographic variables. A person's views on religion can also change throughout the course of a life—and can even pivot through the attitudinal circumstances of a week or a day. During an interview with *Time* magazine, asked whether he believed in a supernatural God, the psychologist Robert Coles replied, "Sometimes I do, and at other times I have my moments of doubt."[2]

We have seen how interpreters relate to religious facts with very different purposes and styles. To some, religion is strictly an object to be analyzed, to others a voice to be listened to, and to others a message to be announced. The stance one takes toward an object naturally conditions the way the object appears.[3] One even thinks here of warning proverbs like, "When the anthropologists arrive, the gods flee," or "the watched pot never boils." So the different intentions of the interpreters generate different contexts of meaning.

This is the so-called hermeneutical circle, that what we say about any object is already interwoven with what we have asked and assumed about it.[4] The situation of the interpreter already preconditions the possible range or kind of religion that will be selected and seen. We cannot see in religion the categories that we have not already recognized in our world or in ourselves.

Audience as Context

Language implies audience, and interpretation is also a form of communication, a social act. We speak and write according to the perceived needs of those with whom we are communicating. Part of the nature of language is that there is a receiver on the other end of it. We interpret for one set of listeners or readers rather than others. We reinterpret classic texts in terms of shifting contemporary issues. There is not only a sociology of religion, but a sociology of the interpretation of religion.

To whom, then, are we interpreting religion? If interpretation means connecting with a particular group's expectations, capacities, and questions, and if to explain something is to explain it *to* someone, then who the someone is and what their preconceptions of religions are is a crucial factor in the interpretive process. Are we addressing a congregation which expects religion to be applied to individual lives? Are we speaking to an academic profession that is evaluating one's theories in terms of objective accuracy, or in terms of whether they display proper tenurable intellectual rigor? Are we engaging a classroom of students who favor no particular faith but expect sheer information, Socratic challenge, or entertainment? Are we confiding secretly with a friend about our own beliefs? Are we working out a theory that will be respectable to readers committed to scientific method? When asked whether he thought Moses wrote the first five books of the Bible, a rabbinical scholar who was conversant with both orthodox and secular views of authorship immediately responded, "It depends on who is asking the question."

We saw in the previous chapter that some insiders explicitly declare that religious explanations should correlate with what the listener is "ready" to hear. Yet even at the everyday level people match their language to the situation and needs of those with whom they are speaking. The audience supplies the cues, the questions, the responsiveness, the level of comprehension. To a sophisticated Greek readership, for whom the literal readings of the Bible would be an embarrassment, the Hellenistic Jewish philosopher Philo of Alexandria interpreted the stories of the Exodus from Egypt, the desert wandering, and the coming to the promised land as allegories of the liberation, trials, and homecoming of the individual soul. Modern film producers have been known to withdraw and revise movie endings to satisfy the tastes of viewers.

There are indeed countless interpretations of religion, but to most readers they are completely irrelevant because they are geared to some audience other than themselves. Rows and rows of religion books sit side by side on libraries' shelves, mutually impertinent to each other's form of knowledge. They belong to different interpretive communities, different circles of conversation.

If the scale creates the phenomenon, the audience is surely part of the scale.

The Varying Object of Interpretation

What about the object of interpretation? Whatever the contextuality of interpreter and audience, the most important factor in any interpretation is its supposed object, that is, the thing it is trying to interpret. We will devote more attention to this.

Because of the circular character of interpretation, one could argue that not only does the scale create the phenomenon, but that the phenomenon creates the scale. The evidence which interpretation selects to interpret is already the beginning of the interpretation. Which part of the city have we chosen to talk about? Which view of Mount Fuji? Which aspect of Mr. Jones's church-going behavior? Which function of the symbol "Christ?" The choices start to determine the level of explanation.

This initial act of selection contextualizes the question of the meaning of the object. If we ask, "How do you interpret 'God?' " the way the object is posed here already implies some reference to biblical associations. A careful answer would have to address what is meant by "God" in the question in order to say what "God" means. Which god? To whom? It is the same with any aspect of religion or with religion in general. Which religion? According to whom? On which angle are we focusing? What is it about religion that is unclear? What, exactly, is the text to be explained?

Any religion contains an inexhaustible number of behaviors and images, each forming a different context of meaning for its adherents, according to shifting circumstances. Which of these, then, have we chosen to view? Here is a description of the ritual mound which is built in front of every house in a certain West African village:

> The earthen *lisenpo* mound in front of the house door . . . represents . . . the great altar of Kuiye, the solar deity. It also recalls the altar dedicated to this deity at Linaba, the mythical village of creation. It serves additionally as an Earthly shrine for Kuiye and his Earthly complement, Butan. This mound symbolizes at the same time the soul or life force of the house and its members. It is identified, in turn, as a reference to the past family members and to lineage unity and division. Furthermore, the *lisenpo* mound is an essential symbol of house political autonomy and power. In this

way, like a telegraph wire, it carries a diversity of messages simultaneously. It is clearly multiplex. Rather than indicating contradiction, these meanings reflect the multivalent character of Batammaliba symbolic and metaphoric forms. [5]

To interpret these mounds—the objects might indeed have no meaning whatsoever to an uninformed outsider—we would clearly have to be careful about which function of them we were addressing.

Every Batammaliba house also has horns posted at the entryway. Their meanings, too, are varied and contextual.

In cosmological contexts, the horns are associated with ordered movement of the sun back and forth across the sky each day and year. On other occasions, the horns are identified as altars to Kuiye, the deity whose daily and yearly passage they mark. From the perspective of human anatomy, they suggest testicles, the source of the fertilizing sperm that, like Kuiye, is necessary for new life. In the context of the family, the horns serve as metaphors for the husband and wife and for the succession of generations. As a major designator of gender differences in game, the horns reinforce the division between house men and women. In the context of house security, the horns recall the protection and power associated with the hunted game. They are accordingly an important referent to house autonomy. In funerary contexts, in turn, the horns serve as important metaphors of death and the associated transition of the deceased elder's soul. [6]

Which horns are we interpreting?

Other kinds of examples illustrate other aspects of the shifting religious object. On 18 November 1978, 914 members of the group known as the Peoples Temple performed mass suicide in Jonestown, Guyana. The event immediately became a news phenomenon. Public response was that the episode signified a horrible, telling example of how a crazed religious leader can brainwash and coerce followers.

Yet again, what Jonestown "is" as an object depends on the questions "To whom?" and "Which aspects of it?" [7] To the ordinary newspaper reader, who is already suspicious of self-styled sect leaders, the meaning of Jonestown is all too clear on the surface. What that reader sees is two pieces of data: the fact of the suicide and the fact that the leader commanded the followers to perform it. This information becomes the sole object and hence basis of interpretation.

At the same time, a fair reconstruction of the significance of Jonestown for its participants would show other meanings of the event. To the adherents, most of whom were nonwhite, the occasion to some extent represented a sacred act of martyrdom that defied the values of a racist society. If the Peoples Temple movement is seen in terms of what it meant to its believers, it must be understood in terms of the problems in the world that it was trying to overcome. Thus one suicide note read, "Jim Jones showed us all this—that we could live together with our differences—that we were all the same—human beings;" others spoke of Jonestown as "the most peaceful, loving community that had eliminated racism, sexism, elitism," and of how "we died because you would not let us live."[8] At the individual level, and completely apart from any judgments that can be made about the leader, many members had in fact had their lives changed by Jones's teaching and charisma. They had overcome heroin addictions and other desperate family and personal problems. They freely chose to join the group, and once within it, expressed their gratitude through obedience. Of that fact the newspapers and their readers were oblivious. They were more interested in the voices of the disenchanted sect members, for whom the enterprise had become a scandal, than in reconstructing the world of the ordinary believer, for whom it was an attempt to overcome the values of a dehumanizing society. Nor was the public interpreter interested in the historical or comparative patterns in which giving one's life for a higher cause could be construed as in some ways normal religious behavior.

A coercion phenomenon suggests a coercion explanation. An antiracism phenomenon suggests an antiracism explanation. A self-sacrifice phenomenon suggests a self-sacrifice explanation.

When the object of interpretation comes clothed in language, the interpretation has already begun. The words—was she kidnapped or was she rescued?—and their inevitable associations become the interpreters. Things and events, people and histories, come wrapped in linguistic resonances, and certainly most of the history of religion is accessible to us only through the recapitulations and phrasings of language. To speak of "Jesus" has a range of associations different than speaking more theologically of "the Christ." Every government, political party, news broadcaster, debater, and parent knows and practices the phenomenon of putting an interpretive spin on language in order to control the response to it. In arenas of conflict each side construes the opposite side in negative terms ("they believe in abortion;" "they believe women don't have the right to choose") and perceives its own position in positive terms ("pro-life," "pro-choice"). The terms posit the datum.

Like history itself, religious life is in motion. It is part of an ongoing process where the present is always a little different, because the past is constantly being added to, and thus always recontextualizing the present. There is always some reconfiguration of circumstances, and hence of meaning. The object we are explaining is on the move, however imperceptibly. The Peoples Temple and its founder were different phenomena in the late sixties than they were in the late seventies. The text does not stand still, and it has been argued that interpretation therefore cannot either.[9] When we are explaining something religious, we need to take this movement into account, to clarify which moment of it we are singling out.

Varieties and Paradoxes of Religiousness. Having returned now to the initial question of the intrinsic elasticity of religion as an object, we can see how very different characterizations of religiousness have come into play. Religiousness: is it becoming possessed by a god, is it strict adherence to a taboo, or is it care for others? We have already seen that it has been connected with either end of the polarities of order and freedom, tradition and innovation, nostalgia and rebellion, home and abandoning home. To those surrounded by chaos, it may connect with the conserving, centripetal forces of order and territory; while to those held captive by society, it may associate with the loosening forces of liberation and transcendence. Religiousness binds and unbinds, separates and brings together, maintains discipline and invites ecstasy. An Eskimo shaman said that "all true wisdom is only to be learned far from the dwellings of men, out in the great solitudes."[10] Yet the great tradition of Confucianism with its principle of social reciprocity is built on the very reversal of this, namely that we learn wisdom through perfecting social relationships.

Any of the following five aspects of religiousness could be the basis for a different theory.

One type of religiousness takes place through the medium of ecstatic, emotional experience. It uses the fervor of enhanced feeling and vitality to convey participation in the sacred. The intensity of the sacred is approached through the intensity of experience. Ecstasy, literally "standing outside oneself," transports the adherent into a nonordinary state of consciousness. Triggers for activating the state may be singing, dancing, or even the use of psychedelic substances. Religion is contact with spirit. If this is what we mean by religion, it is not difficult to see how psychological explanations of the "need" for self-transcendence, or spiritualistic explanations of the existence of other realms of consciousness, address the selected data.[11]

A second type of religiousness is associated with contemplative wisdom and introspection. Here is a realm not of effervescence and trance, but of composure, mindfulness, and insight. The object is not to go out of oneself but to collect oneself. If this is religion, we may expect a very different interpretive frame than that based on supernatural ecstasy or activity.

A third image of religiousness is based on the phenomena of sacrifice and asceticism—the deliberate renunciation of self-gratification. This is the way of purification, expiation, and penitence—deprofanizing one's life so as to achieve sanctity. Is this the essence of religion? If so, we might turn to theories of the sublimation of violence and guilt, or the need to take self-produced evil seriously.[12]

In contrast is a fourth mode, the ethical. Here religiousness is expressed in relationships between people. The virtues of caring, love, compassion, forbearance, charity, mercy, and understanding are the vehicles of religious fulfillment. Good deeds become the mark of a religious person. Impressive examples of compassion here parallel feats of asceticism: while some religious people strip their lives of all self-possession in isolated hermitages, others spend their lives attending the wounds of the sick. If religion is responsibility for "the other," we would need still another, entirely different theory than those just mentioned. The primordial religious fact might be the "I-Thou" relation.[13]

Finally, many would equate religiousness with faith, in any of its several versions—belief, trust, submission, obedience, fidelity, or receptivity.[14] Often the question of religion for those who face secular culture is simply the question of belief, and many theories of religion concentrate on arguments either for or against the validity of the belief in God.

These types are but a sampling. The point is that one's concept of religiousness is based on certain examples, but the examples in turn derive from one's concept. The complexity of religious life and the variability of the religious object are thus analogous to the variety of activities that might conceivably be considered under the rubric of athletic life: how different would be theories of sport based respectively on running, swimming, throwing, jumping, catching, hitting, or shooting.

Interpreting religion is a relative matter, not because there is nothing out there corresponding to it, but because there is so much out there that our concepts of it are necessarily limited to highly situated choices.

Reflecting on Contextuality

Much of the next chapter addresses this heading, so I will be brief at this point.

To reflect upon interpretation is to identify its purposes, its settings, and its selections. It is to be attentive to the reciprocal relationship between the interpreter's world and the choices of religious things interpreted.

Context is of course not all there is to say about interpretation. Surely testing the content of an interpretation by sifting relevant evidence is a process of central concern to all those affected by the consequences of any given explanatory frame.

Yet unless we fathom the shifting, defining role of context, we can scarcely begin to understand what we are doing when we talk about religion. Unless we see the contexts of other views, we cannot see their text, and we will scarcely be self-conscious of our own. Understanding the comparative contextuality of interpretation has some of the same value as the process of understanding "other" religions or worldviews. Only when we see how our own interpretive place differs from others in the range of possible settings can we appreciate what is distinctive about it. It comes down to something like knowing our place in the landscape, in the shadows of Mount Fuji or Dublin.

The concept of plural contexts moves us out of the old two-option turf—in which biblical religion and Western science vie to represent the real world—to a wider universe of multiplicity. It helps overcome some of the contentiousness of single-model, totalizing views of the world, and suggests images of the coexistence of meanings. With the exhaustion of the idea that any one interpretation represents the final truth about the world, or that any one method for organizing and explaining data is absolute, interpretation itself remains always open, self-questioning, and on the move.

In a conceptual universe that is both plural and moving, where interpretation itself becomes the subject matter, any interpreter of interpretation will need to be versatile and conceptually multilingual. Applied to the understanding of religion, the capacity to see through many eyes and from many viewpoints—a capacity that is not necessarily tantamount to agreeing with the theories based on those viewpoints—would seem to be indispensable. The multiplicity of interpretive frames is not only a fact of our public life and social coexistence, but inevitably a revelation of the many-faceted nature of the subject matter itself.

8

Plurality: Issues and Implications

It is time to consider at least briefly some of the broader questions about the coexistence of interpretations and some of the results of this pluralistic approach.

The Question of Compatibility

To what extent do the different coexisting views contradict each other or fit together? Is it enough just to assume that they sit peaceably side by side, and that they are only parallel rather than contending universes? When does coexistence become mutual denial?

In the simplest sense, contradiction occurs when there is a common object incompatibly interpreted: *either* that is my dog over there across the street *or* it is not. The Shroud of Turin is either from the first century C.E. or it is not. In either case it is conventionally agreed that these objects exist, so that their identification as belonging to a certain owner or century can be verified by standard procedures. Misinterpretation or error is possible. The lake can be shown to be a mirage.

Yet interpretive issues in religion are rarely so evidential. "Christ" is not an agreed-upon object that simply requires historical or textual verification, but is already itself an interpretive symbol. When we move from the realm of facts (Whose dog is it? What percent of the American population has been baptized?) to the realm of meanings (What is the significance of religion? What is the meaning of my life? Is the Qur'an divinely ordained?), the

125

issue is not one of verifiability but of perspective, not a question of proving an object's existence but of affirming what it is to mean.

Conflict in interpreting religion, then, is more a consequence of disparate perspectives than of disparate facts. If the theist says "God made the world," and the physicist says, "No, the world was made from a hydrogen explosion," and the neopagan says, "The world is the body of a great goddess," there is no common factual object here to verify, like the dog across the street. The world is itself the question mark. It is that which comes to us only through interpretation. We do not have an uninterpreted world with which to compare these interpreted worlds in order to ascertain whether they are "true" or not.[1] If the theist does not admit the existence of the vacant world as depicted by the materialist, and the materialist does not admit the existence of a divine creation as depicted by the theist, then there is no common "it" to disagree about except the use of the word *world.*

The same goes for the term *religion.* We have seen that there is no bare evidence, no set of uninterpreted facts that can tell us what religion is.[2] Religion, like the world, is not an object that we have access to apart from our descriptions of it, but an object already formed by our definitions of it. The question of which interpretation of religion is right remains unanswerable without recourse to the implied authority of one's own interpretive frame.

Perspectives existing side by side do not necessarily conflict until they start denying each other. If we only affirm our own view and do not deny others, we live in harmless seclusion. But as soon as we say, "Christ is the only way to God," or "social explanation of religion is the only valid explanation," or "the preacher is only out to make money," we enter public territory and we challenge other people's models. It is not what we affirm, but what we deny, that makes all the trouble.

The denial of other views is typically a consequence of the need to protect or affirm one's own. We reject other views when the truth of our own does not appear to be acknowledged in them. If one blind man believes the elephant is like a tree and another that it is like a wall, then the reason they argue is not because they understand the alternative accounts and reject them, but rather in order to defend their own respective beliefs. The blind men are not even aware of each other's different experiences. None of them have the slightest idea about how their counterparts are relating to the elephant or why they say what they do.

A different form of conflict is the approach of theories that are specifically constructed to replace the inadequacies of previous ones. We have seen the acute, adversarial element in most critical interpretations of religion. The critics are sounding the alarm against old ways of seeing religion, and their rhetoric is strong and exaggerated in order to call attention to what they have discovered that had not been said or seen before. The sociological, psychological, and comparative approaches that we reviewed also arose out of a need to give systematic attention to aspects of religion that other theories had neglected. Even certain religious interpretations were designed to create deeper, less superficial explanations of their own traditions. Alternative interpretations of religion—whether those of insiders or outsiders—could thus be said to form a kind of interdependent environment. What each says is typically contrastive, correctional, or supplemental to what the others around it have or have not said. Each stakes out a territory in relation to the current, operating geography of interpretation.

But if on the one hand some views are superficially incompatible because of their intrinsically conflictive nature, on the other hand there are instances where views can easily go together. These are cases where the approaches describe different aspects of the same general object, or look at that object through simply different but noncontentious vocabularies. What is called salt can also, compatibly, be looked at as sodium chloride.

In this regard it is useful to think of the human being as a model referent of multiple interpretations. We have already used the examples of the elephant and Mr. Jones to show how plural views may be conjoined if they correspond to plural aspects of the same referent. Consider now a fuller instance.

An Example. Imagine a pilgrim climbing on her knees to a shrine. What is it that we see? If we are unaware passersby, we may note erroneously what we take to be a physically disabled person, unable to use her legs. If we are critics of religion in general, we may automatically see an instance of dupery and ignorance, or compulsive self-punishment, or social oppression. If we are sociologists or anthropologists, we may see an observance that functions to integrate individuals from socially marginal classes into the power and values of a central collective institution. If we are

Jungians, we may see a person acting out a search for selfhood through the process of humbling the ego and through the symbolism of ascending a hill (the self). If we are scholars of comparative religion, we may see a ritual reenactment of a Christian myth and a local version of the universal pattern of pilgrimage behavior. If we are non-Catholic Christians whose traditions do not include such devotions, we may contemptuously see the superstitions of a rival faith; but if we are Hindus, we might observe a common, normal form of religious expression. If we are Christian mystics, we may see in the woman's face a oneness with the face of Christ and in her actions the passion of Christ. If we are in an airplane, we may have trouble from that distance seeing the woman at all, and she may look more like an ant. If we are evolutionists, we may admire what an interesting creature the Paleozoic, Devonian fish turned out to be.[3]

By varying frames of imaging we may see victimage, irony, loneliness, beauty, illusion, incarnation, heroism, comedy, and pathos. Is there any limit to what one might observe? A photographer taking pictures of the woman might capture her presence in endless interpretive moments, thus giving us limitless visual messages from every angle, each shot capturing a different view through close-ups or side views, through the use of backgrounds and body motions, through a bit of disheveled hair or some other expressive emphasis.[4] The very fact that the woman can be so seen, that she can become a photograph and hence a framed, fixed object to be contemplated or speculated about, produces an additional interpretive context of its own. And cameras aside, any observer, with the human eye, may see here something never even seen before, and never to be seen again—may see things that never become part of any theory at all.

And who knows what Martha (let us realize that she has a name) herself is seeing? Were she to be interviewed as to her self-perceptions, we might even be surprised ("It's just become a habit—I do it every year," or "I enjoy the pilgrimage retreat—it's a chance to get away from my job and be with my friends in the country"), or otherwise enlightened by professed religious intentions ("I am doing this in gratitude for my recovery from cancer," or "My love of Christ is such that I want to participate in his agony," or "I am doing this sheerly as a devotion for my deceased parents in purgatory").

Finally, self-conscious students of interpretation might even want to ask why in the first place our eye gravitated to the woman rather than to some other object, or for that matter what it means that this particular example has been selected here rather than another.

What are we to make of this assemblage of views?

First, it is clear that some could be corroborated by evidence. For example, it is determinable that Martha is not on her knees because she is incapable of walking, and that compared with human beings she is not an ant. The psychological, sociological, and mythological patterns at work could be checked by evidence and counterevidence from those respective contexts.

As for the claims that Martha is a fool or a saint, no objective evidence will settle the matter. This is an area of judgment, not of data. Here is the realm of what William James called one's "over-beliefs," the worldviews we choose to live by but for which no evidence or proof is possible or conclusive. Some interpretations, that is, are not controlled scientific hypotheses but acts of seeing. The religious mystic's interpretation is itself a religious act, just as the skeptic's interpretation is itself a skeptical act. The photographer's angle-setting is a perceptual act. Martha's choice of words and images to describe her observances on the hill is an act of self-definition.

The different views can seem jarring on the surface when taken all at once. Some of them are incompatible in the sense that they cannot occupy the same space at the same time. But the important qualifier here is, "at the same time."

For if the views are taken sequentially they fall into their own intelligible places, describing different aspects of the object. As such, they are not contradictory because the points they make are all made in varying, successive milieux and are relative to the way the point is contextualized in those frames. An elephant can be like a wall, and then like a rope, and then like a tree. From a great distance Martha is in many ways like an ant. The image is not absurd, and in the large scale of time her limbs are indeed viewable as latter-day transformations of Paleozoic fins. Martha is a piece of social fabric, an instance of Christian patterning, a manifestation of certain global religious types, and a unique biographical story. She is an insider to herself, but in shifting ways, and she is a statistical object. She is all foolishness to some, all saintliness to others.

The example of Martha suggests a kind of ecology of perception. To each interpreter the object seen ineluctably corresponds to a meaningful datum or category in the viewer's world.

While certain viewpoints may actually be intended to reduce the meaning of Martha to a single view (combatively, "it's pretense only," or piously, "she does this purely for devotion to God"), others are not exclusivistic. Some views are intended as complementary or partial rather than all-encompassing. For example, the comparativist's perspective usually assumes that a religious phenomenon is a composite or integration of historical, social, and other factors, and that human life is nested in a series of overlapping, interwoven matrices, each analyzable on its own terms yet contributing to a picture of the whole. It is also conceivable that some religious views could see Martha in terms of a kind of unified field theory. Thus in chapter 6 we considered certain capacious religious models that pictured humans as multileveled beings (e.g., physical, rational, and spiritual), having a hierarchy of needs. Some such schemas propose "a full spectrum view of the human condition in its secular as well as divine possibilities," arguing that the social science and religious viewers are each by themselves only "half-sighted."[5]

Is there a best view of Martha? A whole picture that can be defended as offering more explanatory power or understanding than others? Yet again, "more explanatory" according to what criterion? For purposes of what kind of understanding? To think of the many views of Martha as adding up to a singular, composite picture is possible only if one acknowledges that the picture is itself another view, an interpretive whole geared to one paradigm or another.

It is at this point that the lesson of the elephant stops, or at least points to another set of questions. For the teller and for the audience of that parable, the story conveniently visualizes an object that the blind men themselves cannot see, whereas in figuring how views of religion add up this is scarcely the analogy. We have seen that religion—or for that matter the world in which Martha dwells—is not a visibly agreed-upon object that has a certain final shape. It is not a form we would all see identically if we just composed the available pieces of our own world puzzles. We do not have a completed picture of the puzzle on the cover of the box—as we do with the elephant—as a guide for the task of fitting everything together. In construing the available, possible resources for interpreting religion, we and our cultures have become the makers of the picture, so that we have Buddhist-shaped elephants as well as Freudian- and Jungian-shaped elephants, Catholic-shaped Marthas and Durkheim-shaped Marthas. The question of Martha becomes the question of human existence. To the interpreter, what ultimately looms behind the pieces of any Martha—of any religion, of any world—will be named by the symbols that unify or cap off the viewer's own conception and experience of the world, drawn from the language of science, or of culture, or of selfhood, or of despair, or of the gods.

The Reciprocity Model

In this study we have been less concerned to cover all theories than to concentrate on the formative, selective relationship between type of seeing and type of subject matter seen. Plurality has yielded an important principle: the reciprocity of frame and object, perception and reality.

An interpretive paradigm has connected all of the above chapters, and has informed the presentation of each set of material. It is a perspectival model that provides a certain interpretation of interpretation, and in doing this it forms an alternative to two traditional views of knowledge. The first is the objectivist view that reality is "there" and humans can either truthfully represent it or not, either through science or religion. In objectivism the world is whatever it is, independent of any subjective angle on it. Religiously speaking, God is "there," independent of our perception, and scientifically speaking, matter and energy are "there," independent of our perception. The second traditional model, or subjectivism, is that there is nothing there to know, and all human interpretation is more or less made up. It is whistling in the dark. Our representations do not correspond to anything. This is also called skepticism or strict relativism.

In contrast, the reciprocity model suggests that the world "gives" itself to humans in the very act of interpretation. Whether scientifically or religiously, we receive the world according to the framework or equipment of our understanding. The reciprocity model focuses on the point at which we construe any object, and shows how that object appears in correlation with the way it is conceived or experienced. "Reality" here is mediated by interpretation, by experience. That is, to perceive any object is to perceive it or experience it *as* something.[6] The world "is," then, what it is "experienced as."[7] Religious experience is one among many ways of experiencing the world, and even within religion there are innumerable world-descriptions.

The force of this relational point of view is that it acknowledges the relativity of reality to human constructs of it, without denying that there is anything outside of our own views. It forthrightly assumes that there is more to the world than what any one view sees. The world and its objects, then, are not just fiction, not merely "constructed" in the sense of wholly made up. Rather they are constructed in the sense of being constituted or given shape by interpretive frames and acts.[8] Meaning is not "just" self-made; it is the connection humans make with objects, wherein part of the object shows itself back to us in meaningful terms.

The concept of relationality therefore takes a middle way. It sticks just to those points where the meanings and images of the world are generated, and notes that we have a role in forming those meanings. This experiential middle realm acknowledges both the scientific act of organizing data and the religious act of faith. The world becomes known through its own various symbolic frames.

The reciprocity concept is not just a way of explaining theories about religion. We saw that it is also a model for the way religion itself takes place for its participants. It is significant that every major interpretive approach has acknowledged that various kinds of religion are correlative with various kinds of human positionings. As the followers, so the gods.

Whether seen from without or within, religion is therefore like the shape-changing sea god Proteus, who "will reply only to the question put to him, and what he discloses will be great or trivial, according to the question asked."[9] The subject matter reflects back to us the nature of our question and makes us accountable for it, and self-consciousness about the equipment we use is not the least of the lessons of the reciprocity paradigm.

Interpretation as Act. By focusing on reciprocity, we shift emphasis from intellectual representations of reality (Are they true? Are they false?) to interpretive practices or acts—acts of selecting or situating reality according to the positioning, purposes, and needs of the interpreter.

Interpretation is an act of language, with its roots in speech.[10] When we talk about religion we are not just thinking something, but doing something, and what we do is performed in an interactive setting. Theory is a form of practice.

If interpretations are seen this way, they can be judged not only by their use of evidence, but also by their appropriateness to culturally defined issues, settings, and values. Concepts, we have seen, go with contexts and audiences, where they are either in place or out of place. They belong with times, places, and interpretive communities. Some communities need to deal with questions of how to understand or speak of religious truths; others, where issues of self, gender, or social understanding are normative or urgent, need different interpretive frames. The questions create the interpretive tasks. The questions create the answers.

Facing a New Relativity

Clearly we are dealing here with some kind of relativity. Though elaborate philosophical debates have taken place over relativism as a position,[11] this is not the place to enter fully into them. Let us clarify, however, the kind of relativity this book represents and the kind it does not.

To many, *relativism* is a negative, even fearful word, a term of denial. It implies the absence of standards, the rejection of any common truth. It appears as a conceptual and moral nihilism. It connotes that all views about the world are of equal value. It implies that anything goes. It even appears to be a logically fallacious view, because it makes an exception to its own position: the very assertion of relativism is itself nonrelativistic. Some claim that it represents a worldview that is insipid and toothless—a passive pluralism that "masks a genial confusion in which one tries to enjoy the pleasures of difference without ever committing oneself to any particular vision of resistance and hope."[12] Its view that views about the world are "only" someone's point of view appears simplistic and cheap.

I do not believe these problems and negations represent the viewpoint of this study, where the factor of relativity emerges as an occasion for understanding rather than as a position of denial. Relativity—a useful term indeed—here describes the way different languages and positions give different textures to the world. The notion of the relationality of frame to object is an affirmation of procedural comprehension rather than of metaphysical attribution and despair. It is a practical model for understanding the world of interpretation, not an objective assertion about the nature of the world. It is not a fixed position itself, but a working model for fathoming the nature of positionality. It is not about the absence of meaning, but the formation of meaning.

Relativity here, then, is positive, not negative. It affirms the role of frameworks in shaping objects, rather than denying that frameworks refer to anything real. It does not say that everything is "merely" in the interpreter's mind, or that the world is "only" in the eye of the beholder, but does assume that the world is a huge, multilayered affair, and that the interpreter selects from it, configures it, and receives aspects of it. Its import is not to deny common knowledge, but to acknowledge and clarify difference. Far from creating a scene where nothing matters, it is a notion that could help us become self-reflective and accountable for our interpretive language and acts. It is a lesson in humility.

It is quite possible to acknowledge the relativity of perspectives while still maintaining one's own individual standards and choices regarding what is of value in the world and what principle or principles will guide one's thought and social actions. It may be that one's view includes the idea that other views than one's own are inadequate. Understanding the relativity of interpretations does not in itself imply that one cannot make judgments or have one's own absolutes. This makes all the more sense if interpretations of religion are understood as agendas for ways one chooses to see the world, rather than as final truths that literally represent it.

Such methodological pluralism[13] is itself a culturally located view and method. It has its purposes—to come to terms with the disparity of world pictures and world knowledges, with the logic of different viewpoints, with the world-construction process, with the otherwise captivating role of single frames, with the invention and, paradoxically, the discovery of religion as an object. Perhaps one day such issues will recede, but today they have a certain cultural and educational urgency.

We hear the modern situation described as being awash in a sea of meanings, yet the boundlessness of interpretation is not necessarily a sign of metaphysical chaos. It is a plurality that can itself be "read," that can itself become a subject matter, that can educate us to the process of how we see things and why any given world appears the way it does.

If so, the relativity which once seemed to be such a threatening abyss, such a loss of world, may become a clarifying lesson in how the world takes place.

Religion and Existence

Ultimately, the question of religion and the question of existence are connected. As we think about the one we will think about the other. Religion embodies the question of the nature of the world. We cannot think of it in terms other than the terms in which we think about ourselves.

As with the world, there are endless contexts in which to view religion, and endless questions to ask of it. What sort of an affair are we in? What kind of thing, after all, is a human being? What do we choose to see about ourselves? With the visible world in front of us, what features do we select as real and salient? Do we analyze, or do we behold? Which part of the earth's text do we read? It is safe to say that the history of the world's imagination has not yet exhausted the possible ways of seeing the human situation. There is always another context, another lens, another imagining, another way to thematize the world. Religions themselves are some of those ways.

Interpretation is thus an unlimited resource, and like the world, with which it is intimately connected, is many-layered and many-voiced, each voice in its place, each in its frame, each in its season.

Notes

1. Interpretive Frames

1. Some surveys of approaches to religion are available, such as Eric J. Sharpe, *Comparative Religion: A History*, 2d ed., (La Salle, Ill.: Open Court, 1986); Jacques Waardenburg, *Classical Approaches to the Study of Religion*, vol. 1 (The Hague: Mouton, 1973); and Frank Whaling, ed., *Contemporary Approaches to the Study of Religion*, 2 vols. (Berlin: Mouton, 1984–85). From the anthropological viewpoint, see Brian Morris, *Anthropological Studies of Religion: An Introductory Text* (Cambridge: Cambridge University Press, 1987). A diverse range of standpoints is surveyed in John Bowker, *The Sense of God: Sociological, Anthropological and Psychological Approaches to the Origin of the Sense of God* (Oxford: Clarendon Press, 1973). An anthology with a variety of short selections on interpreting religion is Walter H. Capps, *Ways of Understanding Religion* (New York: Macmillan, 1972); and another reasonable introductory textbook sampling is Robert S. Ellwood, Jr., *Introducing Religion: From Inside and Outside*, 2d ed. (Englewood Cliffs, N.J.: Prentice-Hall, 1983), which has a companion anthology edited by Ellwood, *Readings on Religion: From Inside and Outside* (Englewood Cliffs, N.J.: Prentice-Hall, 1978).

2. The term *postmodern* is sometimes applied to culture that has realized all of its systems of knowledge, including science, to be "constructs" or models. Manifestos of the new self-reflexive outlook in the social sciences are George E. Marcus and Michael M. J. Fischer, *Anthropology as Cultural Critique: An Experimental Moment in the Human Sciences* (Chicago: University of Chicago Press, 1986); and Paul Rabinow and William M. Sullivan, eds., *Interpretive Social Science: A Second Look* (Berkeley: University of California Press, 1987). A useful theological account is Frederic B. Burnham, ed., *Postmodern Theology: Christian Faith in a Pluralist World* (San Francisco: Harper and Row, 1989). In science, the classic is Thomas S. Kuhn, *The Structure of Scientific Revolutions*, 2d ed. (Chicago: University of Chicago Press, 1970). Influential philosophical works have been Richard Rorty, *Philosophy and the Mirror of Nature* (Princeton: Princeton University Press, 1979); and Richard J. Bernstein, *Beyond Objectivism and Relativism: Science, Hermeneutics, and Praxis* (Philadelphia: University of Pennsylvania Press,

1983). See also Walter Watson, *The Architectonics of Meaning: Foundations of the New Pluralism* (Albany: State University of New York Press, 1985).

3. A phrase attributed to the scientist, Henri Poincaré (1854–1912), and often cited by the modern historian of religion, Mircea Eliade.

4. For a rich discussion of the concept of *paradigm* as applied to religious studies, and its relation to both religious imagination and scientific uses, see Garrett Green, *Imagining God: Theology and the Religious Imagination* (San Francisco: Harper and Row, 1989). "The function of religious imagination," Green writes, "is to tell us 'what the world is like' in its broadest and deepest sense" (79). A still useful earlier work is Ian G. Barbour, *Myths, Models and Paradigms: A Comparative Study in Science and Religion* (New York: Harper and Row, 1974).

5. "One hears exacting scholars, as I did at a recent Smithsonian consultation, casually remark with the authority of the commonplace that the epistemological grounding of a physicist's quarks and a Homer's gods is exactly the same." George A. Lindbeck, "The Church's Mission to a Postmodern Culture," in Burnham, *Postmodern Theology*, 51.

6. A highly useful history of the term is given in Wilfred Cantwell Smith, *The Meaning and End of Religion: A New Approach to the Religious Traditions of Mankind* (New York: Macmillan, 1963), chap. 2. My summary is based on Smith's work.

7. Cf. William E. Paden, *Religious Worlds: The Comparative Study of Religion* (Boston: Beacon Press, 1988).

8. John Berger, *Ways of Seeing* (New York: Viking Press, 1973), 8.

9. Nelson Goodman states this well:

> The eye comes always ancient to its work, obsessed by its own past and by old and new insinuations of ear, nose, tongue, fingers, heart, and brain. It functions not as an instrument self-powered and alone, but as a dutiful member of a complex and capricious organism. Not only how but what it sees is regulated by need and prejudice. It selects, rejects, organizes, discriminates, associates, classifies, analyzes, constructs. It does not so much mirror as take and make; and what it takes and makes it sees not bare, as items without attributes, but as things, as food, as people, as enemies, as stars, as weapons. Nothing is seen nakedly or naked.

Languages of Arts: An Approach to a Theory of Symbols (Indianapolis: Bobbs-Merrill Co., 1968), 7–8.

10. For an anthropological treatment of this point see John B. Carroll, ed., *Language, Thought and Reality: Selected Writings of Benjamin Lee Whorf* (Cambridge: MIT Press, 1964).

Also on the idea that language is not an embellishment but a form of perception and action, see George Lakoff and Mark Johnson, *Metaphors We Live By* (Chicago: University of Chicago Press, 1980).

11. The word *interpretation* is from the Latin, where an *interpres* was "an agent between two parties, a negotiator, broker, expounder." The prefix *inter-*, of course, means "between;" but there is some obscurity about *pres*. Some link it with *pretium*, "value, price;" others (*The Oxford English Dictionary*), with a root corresponding to Sanskrit *prath-*, "to spread abroad."

The study of interpretation, known as hermeneutics (from the Greek verb, *hermeneuein*, "to interpret"), today constitutes a vast, often interdisciplinary field. For a general treatment see Richard E. Palmer, *Hermeneutics: Interpretation Theory in Schleiermacher, Dilthey, Heidegger and Gadamer* (Evanston, Ill.: Northwestern University Press, 1969). A good collection of basic texts is found in David E. Klemm, ed. *Hermeneutical Inquiry*, 2 vols. (Atlanta: Scholars Press, 1986). The Greek root of *hermeneutics* has etymological associations with the god Hermes: conveyer of the gods' messages, crosser of boundaries, god of eloquence, and presider over certain forms of popular divination. In Christianity, *hermeneutics* is the branch of theology that deals with the principles of biblical exegesis.

12. A good account of the traditional function of divination is Philip M. Peek, ed., *African Divination Systems: Ways of Knowing* (Bloomington, Ind.: Indiana University Press, 1991).

13. A useful survey of biblical interpretation is Robert M. Grant, with David Tracy, *A Short History of the Interpretation of the Bible*, 2d ed. (Philadelphia: Fortress Press, 1984).

14. A good overview is found in Philip Clayton, *Explanation from Physics to Theology: An Essay in Rationality and Religion* (New Haven: Yale University Press, 1989). A fine applied example of an attempt to take explanatory theory seriously while not reducing religion to the simple, positivistic rules of empirical verification is E. Thomas Lawson and Robert N. McCauley, *Rethinking Religion: Connecting Cognition and Culture* (Cambridge: Cambridge University Press, 1990). A historical account of theories that have tried to explain religion naturalistically is J. Samuel Preus, *Explaining Religion: Criticism and Theory from Bodin to Freud* (New Haven: Yale University Press, 1987).

15. A classic account of the coalescence of interpretation and understanding is Gerardus van der Leeuw, *Religion in Essence and Manifestation*, trans. J. E. Turner (New York: Harper and Row, 1963), especially chapters 107–9.

2. The Challenge

1. *Rationalism* has other meanings in other contexts, for example, in contrast to empiricism. Here I use the term in the context of religious studies, where a rationalist is one who judges religion in terms of its conceptual or rational validity.

2. A theory set forth in his well-known book, *The Golden Bough: A Study in Magic and Religion*, 3d ed., 12 vols. (London: Macmillan, 1911–15).

3. Representative accounts of Nietzsche's views on religion, including *Twilight of the Idols*, *The Anti-Christ*, and *Thus Spoke Zarathustra*, are available in Walter Kaufman, trans., *The Portable Nietzsche* (New York: Viking, 1954).

4. Ludwig Feuerbach, *The Essence of Christianity*, trans. George Eliot (New York: Harper and Row, 1958).

5. A convenient collection of Marx's writings on religion is Karl Marx and Friedrich Engels, *On Religion* (New York: Schocken Books, 1964). For an overview of types of Marxist criticism see Delos B. McKown, *The Classical Marxist Critiques of Religion: Marx, Engels, Lenin, Kautsky* (The Hague: Martinus Nijhoff, 1975).

6. Ibid., 42.

7. Ibid.

8. Ibid.

9. Freud's most direct assessment of religion is his *The Future of an Illusion*, first published in 1927 and available in several editions.

10. More current examples of its applications to religion are Ana-Maria Rizzuto, *The Birth of the Living God: A Psychoanalytical Study* (Chicago: University of Chicago Press, 1979); and the anthropological studies of South Asian religion by Gananath Obeyesekere, *Medusa's Hair: An Essay on Personal Symbols and Religious Experience* (Chicago: University of Chicago Press, 1981), and *The Work of Culture: Symbolic Transformation in Psychoanalysis and Anthropology* (Chicago: University of Chicago Press, 1990).

11. Freud, however, did not invent the idea of the unconscious. For a detailed history of the idea see Henri F. Ellenberger, *The Discovery of the Unconscious: The History and Evolution of Dynamic Psychiatry* (New York: Basic Books, 1970).

12. Sigmund Freud, "Preface," in Theodor Reik, *Ritual: Four Psychoanalytic Studies*, trans. Douglas Bryan (New York: Grove Press, 1962), 10–11.

13. Marx, *On Religion*, 45.

14. Ibid., 50.

15. Given classic exposition by Julius Wellhausen (1844–1918).

16. A useful historical survey of critical studies of the New Testament is Werner Georg Kümmel, *The New Testament: The History of the Investigation of Its Problems*, trans. S. McLean Gilmour and Howard C. Kee (Nashville: Abingdon Press, 1972).

17. For example, see Mary Daly, *Beyond God the Father; Toward a Philosophy of Women's Liberation* (Boston: Beacon Press, 1973).

18. The philosopher Paul Ricoeur distinguished a "hermeneutics of suspicion" (for example, the interpretations of Marx, Nietzsche, and Freud) and a "hermeneutics of retrieval" as two modern forms of interpreting religion. The first shows ways in which religion is something other than what it claims to be. The second recovers or reconstructs religious value out of the texts and symbols of the past.

19. The author of a book that explains religion as an escapist dream dedicates his work to an ancestor "burned at the stake in Abbeville, 1 July, 1766 at the age of eighteen." (Weston La Barre, *The Ghost Dance: Origins of Religion* (Garden City, N.Y.: Doubleday, 1970).

3. As Society, So Religion

1. A respected anthology with a representative sampling of social science positions on religion is W. A. Lessa and E. Z. Vogt, eds., *Reader in Comparative Religion: An Anthropological Approach*, 4th ed. (New York: Harper and Row, 1979). An engagingly written sociological treatment of religion is Peter L. Berger, *The Sacred Canopy: Elements of a Sociological Theory of Religion* (Garden City, N.Y.: Doubleday, 1967). An exemplary general text is Barbara Hargrove, *The Sociology of Religion: Classical and Contemporary Approaches*, 2d ed. (Arlington Heights, Ill.: Harlan Davidson, 1990).

2. Emile Durkheim, *The Elementary Forms of the Religious Life*, trans. Joseph Ward Swain (New York: The Free Press, 1965).

3. This concept has been given clear articulation in Peter Berger's *The Sacred Canopy*.

4. For an exemplary Durkheimian study of the correspondences between concepts of deity and forms of political sovereignty, see Guy E. Swanson, *The Birth of the Gods: the Origin of Primitive Beliefs* (Ann Arbor, Mich: University of Michigan Press, 1960).

5. Durkheim, *Elementary Forms*, 390.

6. Ibid., 391.

7. The concept was developed by the late anthropologist Victor Turner in works like *The Ritual Process* (Chicago: Aldine Publishing Co., 1969).

8. The concept was developed in 1908 by the French anthropologist Arnold van Gennep. See his widely read *Rites of Passage*, trans. Monika B. Vizedom and Gabrielle L. Caffee (Chicago: University of Chicago Press, 1960).

9. A now classic sociology of boundaries and boundary violation is Mary Douglas, *Purity and Danger: An Analysis of Concepts of Pollution and Taboo* (London: Routledge and Kegan Paul, 1966); some of the themes are extended in her *Implicit Meanings: Essays in Anthropology* (London: Routledge

and Kegan Paul, 1975). An important study of the sociology of the purity-impurity polarity in India is Louis Dumont, *Homo Hierarchicus: The Caste System and its Implications*, trans. M. Sainsbury (London: Weidenfeld and Nicolson, 1970).

10. A basic source is Weber's *The Sociology of Religion*, trans. Ephraim Fischoff (Boston: Beacon Press, 1963; first published in German in 1922). Several of the distinctions in this section of the chapter are Weberian.

11. Studies of these include Vittorio Lanternari, *Religions of the Oppressed: A Study of Modern Messianic Cults*, trans. Lisa Sergio (New York: Knopf, 1963), and Bryan R. Wilson, *Magic and the Millennium: A Sociological Study of Religious Movements of Protest Among Tribal and Third-World Peoples* (New York: Harper and Row, 1973).

12. I. M. Lewis, *Ecstatic Religion* (Harmondsworth, England: Penguin Books, 1971), ch. 3.

13. For an illustrative, thoroughgoing socioscientific explanation of supernatural spiritist elements in religion, see the anthropologist Melford Spiro's *Burmese Supernaturalism: A Study in the Explanation and Reduction of Suffering* (Englewood Cliffs, N.J.: Prentice-Hall, 1967).

14. "Reflexive anthropology," or "the observers observed" (to use the title of one work on the subject), does just that. For samples see James Clifford and George E. Marcus, eds., *Writing Culture: The Poetics and Politics of Ethnography* (Berkeley: University of California Press, 1986); George E. Marcus and Michael M. J. Fischer, eds. *Anthropology as Cultural Critique: An Experimental Moment in the Human Sciences* (Chicago: University of Chicago Press, 1986); and James Clifford, *The Predicament of Culture: Twentieth-Century Ethnography, Literature and Art* (Cambridge: Harvard University Press, 1988). For an influential attack on the way Westerners have represented non-Western societies see Edward Said, *Orientalism* (New York: Pantheon, 1978). These positions all look critically at the assumptions of the social scientists and their "inventions" about other cultures, and challenge the notion of fixed, "totalizing," hegemonic paradigms of interpretation. Ethnography is here seen not just as a collection of straight, descriptive knowledge about others, but a creative activity, a genre of writing, fused with the values of the ethnographer's own culture. Naturally the approach is controversial. The analysis of the sociocultural nature of interpretive frames—for example Marxist critiques of the economic and political motivations of the anthropological interpreter, or literary critiques of the "emplotments" or "metanarratives" of Western theorizing—has itself become an industry.

15. Clifford Geertz, *The Interpretation of Cultures: Selected Essays* (New York: Basic Books, Inc., 1973), 5. In Geertz's work a transition from functionalist explanation to the tasks of "understanding" takes place, a transition that has drawn the attention of religion scholars to his writings.

4. As the Psyche, So the Gods

1. An introduction to Jungian thought for the nonspecialist is Carl G. Jung, et al., *Man and His Symbols* (New York: Dell, 1964); of which part 3, by Marie-Louise von Franz, "The Process of Individuation," is an especially accessible overview. Jung's own autobiography, *Memories, Dreams, Reflections* (New York: Random House, 1961), is also a good entree to his ideas. Jung's writings are available in English translation in the *Collected Works of C. G. Jung*, in 19 volumes, published by Princeton University Press. Useful anthologies of his work are Anthony Storr, ed., *The Essential Jung* (Princeton, N.J.: Princeton University Press, 1983), and Joseph Campbell, ed., *The Portable Jung* (New York: Viking Press, 1971).

2. For a comparison of the two figures see Liliane Frey-Rohn, *From Freud to Jung: A Comparative Study of the Psychology of the Unconscious*, trans. Fred E. Engreen and Evelyn K. Engreen (New York: C. G. Jung Foundation, 1974).

3. Jung, *Collected Works*, vol. 9, pt. 1, 56.

4. Jung, *Psychology and Religion* (New Haven: Yale University Press, 1938), 4–5.

5. A classic Jungian account of the correlation of stages of ego development and stages of mythology is Erich Neumann, *The Origins and History of Consciousness*, trans. R. F. C. Hull (Princeton, N.J.: Princeton University Press, 1969; first published in German in 1949).

6. A strongly though not entirely Jungian account of the relation between ego psychology and motifs of the hero-journey is the best-selling work by Joseph Campbell, *The Hero with a Thousand Faces*, 2d ed. (Princeton, N.J.: Princeton University Press, 1968).

7. Campbell, *The Portable Jung*, 648.

8. A classic account of the psychological role of the goddess is Erich Neumann, *The Great Mother: an Analysis of the Archetype*, trans. Ralph Manheim, 2d ed. (Princeton, N.J.: Princeton University Press, 1963).

9. For a treatment of Jung's approach to biblical material see Wayne Rollins, *Jung and the Bible* (Atlanta: John Knox Press, 1983). A key writing of Jung's on the Bible is his *Answer to Job* (anthologized in Campbell, *The Portable Jung*); and much of my representation of his ideas in the following pages draws on that work.

10. Jung, "Answer to Job," 527, 534.

11. Jung, *Collected Works*, vol. 9, pt. 2, *Aion: Researches into the Phenomenology of the Self*, 36–37.

12. Ira Progoff, *The Death and Rebirth of Psychology* (New York: McGraw-Hill, 1973), 183.

13. Jung, *Aion*, 61.

14. From Jung, "The Difference Between Eastern and Western Thinking," in Campbell, *The Portable Jung,* 486.

15. M. Scott Peck's *The Road Less Traveled: A New Psychology of Love, Traditional Values and Spiritual Growth* (New York: Simon and Shuster, 1978), one of the most widely read books of the times, essentially adopts this Jungian model of the relationship of the unconscious and God.

16. A fine work on the way the losses of traditional culture led to increased introspection is Peter Homans, *The Ability to Mourn: Disillusionment and the Social Origins of Psychoanalysis* (Chicago: Chicago University Press, 1989).

17. On this point and on the relation of Jung to postmodernism generally, see Karin Barnaby and Pellegrino D'Acierno, eds., C. G. *Jung and the Humanities: Toward a Hermeneutics of Culture* (Princeton, N.J.: Princeton University Press, 1990); especially the substantive preface by the editors.

18. Jung, *Psychology and Religion,* 114.

19. The most influential neo-Jungian approach is that of James Hillman, whose views may be concisely found in *Archetypal Psychology: A Brief Account* (Dallas: Spring Publications, 1985). A selection of his writings is *A Blue Fire,* ed. Thomas Moore (New York: Harper and Row, 1989). Object-relations theory, which studies the relationship of the ego to objects outside itself (as the matrix within which the psyche is formed), is a development from Freud, but without the antagonism to religion and without the Jungian investment in archetypal theory. Cf. D. W. Winnicott, *Playing and Reality* (New York: Basic Books, 1971); W. W. Meissner, *Psychoanalysis and Religious Experience* (New Haven: Yale University Press, 1984); and H. Kohut, *The Analysis of the Self* (New York: International Universities Press, 1970). Lively feminist critiques are Naomi R. Goldenberg's *Changing of the Gods: Feminism and the End of Traditional Religion* (Boston: Beacon Press, 1979), and *Returning Words to Flesh: Feminism, Psychoanalysis, and the Resurrection of the Body* (Boston: Beacon Press, 1990). See also Christine Downing, *The Goddess: Mythological Representations of the Feminine* (New York: Crossroad, 1984).

5. Comparative Perspective in the Study of Religion

1. Cf. Eric Sharpe, *Comparative Religion: A History,* 2d ed. (La Salle, Ill.: Open Court, 1986); Ninian Smart, *The Phenomenon of Religion* (New York: Herder and Herder, 1973); and Paden, *Religious Worlds.* A valuable resource for the comparative study of religion is Mircea Eliade, ed., *The Encyclopedia of Religion,* 16 vols. (New York: Macmillan, 1987).

2. F. Max Müller, *Lectures on the Science of Religion* (New York: Charles Scribner Co., 1872).

3. Müller adopted the phrase from Goethe, who had applied it to the study of language.

4. Good introductions to Mircea Eliade's work are his *The Sacred and the Profane: The Nature of Religion*, trans. Willard R. Trask (New York: Harcourt, Brace and World, 1959), and *The Quest: History and Meaning in Religion* (Chicago: University of Chicago Press, 1969).

5. Eliade, *The Sacred and the Profane*, 162.

6. Eliade, *The Quest*, 7–8.

7. Mircea Eliade, *Patterns in Comparative Religion*, trans. Rosemary Sheed (Cleveland: World Publishing Co., 1963), xiii.

8. The classic work presenting the phenomenology of religion approach and spelling out its methodology is Gerardus van der Leeuw, *Religion in Essence and Manifestation*.

9. William James, *The Varieties of Religious Experience* (New York: Random House, 1902), 10.

10. Eliade, *The Quest*, 58.

11. For example, Hans H. Penner, *Impasse and Resolution: A Critique of the Study of Religion*, Toronto Studies in Religion, vol. 8 (New York: P. Lang, 1989).

12. For example, Jacques Waardenburg has called for a "new style" phenomenology that is not focused on typologies but on the world of participants. Cf. his *Reflections on the Study of Religion*, Religion and Reason Series, no. 15 (The Hague: Mouton, 1978).

13. As called for in Lauri Honko, ed., *Science of Religion: Studies in Methodology*, Religion and Reason Series, no. 13 (The Hague: Mouton, 1979); and Jonathan Z. Smith, *To Take Place: Toward Theory in Ritual* (Chicago: University of Chicago Press, 1987).

14. The debate over the status of the claim that certain phenomena can be studied as "religious," as distinguished from "social" or "psychological," is represented in the advocate, Daniel L. Pals, "Is Religion a *Sui Generis* Phenomenon?" *Journal of the American Academy of Religion* 55, no. 2 (Fall 1987): 2259–82; and the critics, Robert A. Segal and Donald Wiebe, "Axioms and Dogmas in the Study of Religion," *Journal of the American Academy of Religion* 57, no. 3 (Fall 1989): 591–605.

6. Religious Interpretations of Religion

1. Paul Tillich, *Systematic Theology*, vol. I (Chicago: University of Chicago Press, 1951), 214.

2. A phrase from the introduction of Donald S. Lopez, Jr., ed., *Buddhist Hermeneutics* (Honolulu: University of Hawaii Press, 1988), 8.

3. A prominent Christian theologian, Karl Barth, after carefully considering all the impressive doctrinal similarities between Jesus Christ and the figure of Amida Buddha (as understood by the Pure Land Buddhism tradition of Shinran in Japan) concluded that the "truth of our religion" is ultimately enclosed only in "the one *name* Jesus Christ and nothing else" [emphasis added]. Karl Barth, *Church Dogmatics*, vol. 1, *The Doctrine of the Word of God*, trans. G. T. Thomson and Harold Knight (New York: Charles Scribner's Sons, 1956), 343.

4. For a useful collection of essays on philosophical, cognitive issues about religious language, see Ronald E. Santoni, ed., *Religious Language and the Problem of Religious Knowledge* (Bloomington, Ind.: Indiana University Press, 1968).

5. For a survey see John Macquarrie, *Twentieth Century Religious Thought*, rev. ed. (New York: Charles Scribner's Sons, 1981).

6. Literally "those who know." For an introduction to their approach see Elaine Pagels, *The Gnostic Gospels* (New York: Random House, 1979).

7. For example, see John Hick and Paul F. Knitter, eds., *The Myth of Christian Uniqueness: Toward a Pluralistic Theology of Religions* (Maryknoll, N.Y.: Orbis Books, 1987).

8. John Hick, "Whatever Path Men Choose is Mine," in *Christianity and Other Religions: Selected Readings*, John Hick and Brian Hebblethwaite, eds. (Philadelphia: Fortress Press, 1980), 186.

9. See, for example, John B. Cobb, Jr., *Beyond Dialogue: Toward a Mutual Transformation of Christianity and Buddhism* (Philadelphia: Fortress Press, 1982); Leonard Swidler, *After the Absolute: The Dialogical Future of Religious Reflection* (Minneapolis: Fortress Press, 1990); and John B. Cobb, Jr. and Christopher Ives, eds., *The Emptying God: A Buddhist-Christian-Jewish Conversation* (Maryknoll, N.Y.: Orbis, 1990).

10. Respectively, the approaches of Paul Tillich and Rudolf Otto—the latter known especially for his presentation of this in his classic *The Idea of the Holy*, trans. J. W. Harvey (New York: Oxford University Press, 1958). An impressive recent attempt at a pluralistic theology based on comparative religion material is John Hick, *The Interpretation of Religion: Human Responses to the Transcendent* (New Haven: Yale University Press, 1989).

11. Cf. William Johnston, *The Inner Eye of Love: Mysticism and Religion* (San Francisco: Harper and Row, 1978).

12. An official statement of the Second Vatican Council (1963–65) of the Roman Catholic Church reads: "Those who, through no fault of their own, do not know the Gospel of Christ or his Church, but who nevertheless seek God with a sincere heart, and, moved by grace, try in their actions to do his will as they know it through the dictates of their conscience—those too may achieve eternal salvation." *Vatican Council II: the Conciliar and Post*

Conciliar Documents, ed. Austin Flannery (New York: Costello Publishing Co., 1975, 1984), vol. 1, 367.

13. See, for example, Masao Abe, *Zen and Western Thought*, ed. William R. Lafleur (Honolulu: University of Hawaii Press, 1985).

14. Notably promulgated by the writer Aldous Huxley in his book by that title. Other well known modern exponents are Frithjof Schuon and Huston Smith. For an astute current defense of the model, see Smith's "Is There a Perennial Philosophy?" *Journal of the American Academy of Religion* 55, no. 3 (Fall 1987): 553–66. Also notable is Smith's *Forgotten Truth: The Primordial Tradition* (New York: Harper and Row, 1976).

15. Donald S. Lopez, Jr., and Steven C. Rockefeller, in the introduction to a volume edited by them, *The Christ and the Bodhisattva* (Albany: State University of New York Press, 1987), 36.

16. For a review of current kinds of biblical intepretation see Terence J. Keegan, *Interpreting the Bible* (New York: Paulist Press, 1985). An outstanding work on traditional Jewish hermeneutics is Michael Fishbane, *The Garments of Torah: Essays in Biblical Hermeneutics* (Bloomington, Ind.: Indiana University Press, 1989). A stimulating study of the relation of rabbinic interpretation to modern interpretive theories (of Freud, Lacan, Derrida, and Harold Bloom) is Susan A. Handelman, *The Slayers of Moses: The Emergence of Rabbinic Interpretation in Modern Literary Theory* (Albany: State University of New York Press, 1982).

17. A midrash in Seder Eliyyahu Zuta, cited in Barbara A. Holdrege, "The Bride of Israel: The Ontological Status of Scripture in the Rabbinic and Kabbalistic Traditions," in Miriam Levering, ed., *Rethinking Scripture: Essays from a Comparative Perspective* (Albany: State University of New York Press, 1989), p. 229.

18. R. Eliezar, *Song of Songs Rabbah*, cited in Holdrege, "The Bride of Israel," 229.

19. Gershom G. Scholem, ed., *Zohar: The Book of Splendour* (New York: Schocken Books, 1971), 90.

20. Ibid., 121.

21. Ibid., 122.

22. See Robert M. Grant with David Tracy, *A Short History of the Interpretation of the Bible*, 2d ed. (Philadelphia: Fortress Press, 1984).

23. For a philosophical treatment of the way Zen philosophies can be understood as overcoming some of the concept-bound (or "logocentric") interpretive dilemmas of Western thought, see David Loy, *Nonduality: A Study in Comparative Philosophy* (New Haven: Yale University Press, 1988).

24. Holdrege, "The Bride of Israel," citing *Exodus Rabbah*, 231.

25. Ibid.

26. James Clifford, *The Predicament of Culture* (Cambridge: Harvard University Press, 1989), 145.

27. Cited in Lopez and Rockefeller, *The Christ and the Bodhisattva*, 36.

28. The following summary is based on Thomas P. Kasulis, "Truth Words: The Basis of Kukai's Theory of Interpretation," in Lopez, *Buddhist Hermeneutics*, 257–72.

29. For examples of the pictures, with commentaries, see D. T. Suzuki, *Manual of Zen Buddhism* (New York: Grove Press, 1965), 127–44.

30. I epitomize here the work of Ken Wilber. Quotes are from "Paradigm Wars: An Interview with Ken Wilber," *The Quest* (Spring 1989): 6–19. Representative works of Wilber are *Eye to Eye: The Quest for the New Paradigm*, rev. ed. (Boston: Shambhala Publications, 1990), and *Up from Eden: A Transpersonal View of Human Evolution* (New York: Doubleday, 1981).

31. Eckhart, in C. F. Kelley, *Meister Eckhart on Divine Knowledge* (New Haven: Yale University Press, 1977), 119.

32. Joseph Campbell with Bill Moyers, *The Power of Myth*, ed. Betty Sue Flowers (New York: Doubleday, 1988), 129.

33. For a challenge to the claim that all religions say the same thing, see Keith Ward, "Truth and the Diversity of Religions," *Religious Studies* 26, no. 1 (March 1990): 1–18.

7. The Contextuality of Interpretation

1. The toolbox analogy with language and the important concept that meaning is relative to linguistic usage or even "language games," is an approach elaborated by the influential philosopher Ludwig Wittgenstein (1889–1951). See his *Philosophical Investigations*, trans. G. E. M. Anscombe, 3d ed. (New York: Macmillan, 1968). The pragmatist idea of language as a tool by which we do something about the world, rather than as a picture by which we represent it, has also been well advocated by the contemporary American philosopher Richard Rorty. Rorty sees this as a concept around which such otherwise diverse thinkers as Wittgenstein, John Dewey, and Michel Foucault converge. He notes that "it is useless to ask whether one vocabulary rather than another is closer to reality. For different vocabularies serve different purposes, and there is no such thing as a purpose that is closer to reality than another purpose." Introduction to John P. Murphy, *Pragmatism: From Peirce to Davidson* (Boulder, Colo.: Westview Press, 1990), 3.

2. Richard N. Ostling, "Youngsters Have Lots to Say about God," *Time*, 21 January 1991, 16–17.

3. The way in which every object of consciousness is rendered present by a corresponding act of consciousness has been the subject of much analysis in the tradition of philosophical phenomenology established by the German philosopher Edmund Husserl (1859–1938).

4. The most influential philosophical analysis of this "hermeneutical situation" is by Martin Heidegger (1889–1976), in his famous but difficult *Being and Time*, trans. John Macquarrie and Edward Robinson (New York: Harper and Row, 1962; first published in German in 1927).

5. Suzanne Preston Blier, *The Anatomy of Architecture: Ontology and Metaphor in Batammaliba Architectural Expression* (Cambridge: Cambridge University Press, 1987), 220.

6. Ibid., 221.

7. One of the best and most readable analyses I have seen of the relationship between explaining a phenomenon and understanding the meaning of that phenomenon to the actors involved is Herbert Menzel, "Meaning—Who Needs It?" in Michael Brenner, Peter Marsh, and Marylin Brenner, eds. *The Social Contexts of Method* (New York: St. Martin's Press, 1978), 140–71.

8. David Chidester, *Salvation and Suicide: An Interpretation of Jim Jones, the Peoples Temple and Jonestown* (Bloomington, Ind.: Indiana University Press, 1988), 160.

9. This concept of constantly pivoting, sequential meaning has been effective in the area of literary interpretation. See, for example, Susan Horton, *Interpreting Interpreting: Interpreting Dickens's* Dombey (Baltimore: Johns Hopkins University Press, 1979).

10. Cited in Joan Halifax, *Shamanic Voices: A Survey of Visionary Narratives* (New York: Dutton, 1979), 6.

11. A representative anthropological theory of the origin of religion in ecstatic states is Weston La Barre, *The Ghost Dance: The Origins of Religion* (Garden City, N.Y.: Doubleday, 1970). On the theological side is Rudolf Otto's classic, *The Idea of the Holy*.

12. On sacrifice, see René Girard, *Violence and the Sacred*, trans. Patrick Gregory (Baltimore: Johns Hopkins University Press, 1977). William James interprets asceticism in *The Varieties of Religious Experience*, lectures 11–15.

13. The classic statement about relationship as the basis of religiousness is Martin Buber, *I and Thou*, trans. Ronald Gregor Smith, 2d ed. (New York: Charles Scribner's Sons, 1958).

14. For a fine investigation of the categories of faith and belief in global perspective, see Wilfred Cantwell Smith, *Faith and Belief* (Princeton, N.J.: Princeton University Press, 1979).

8. Plurality

1. The philosopher Nelson Goodman has argued strongly along these lines. See his *Ways of Worldmaking* (Indianapolis: Hackett Publishing Co., 1978).

2. A point stressed in the work of Jonathan Z. Smith; for example, his *Imagining Religion* (Chicago: University of Chicago Press, 1982).

3. I borrow the image from Loren Eiseley, *The Immense Journey* (New York: Vintage Books, 1957), 47–48, where Eiseley speaks of how "a Devonian fish managed to end as a two-legged character with a straw hat."

4. As one observer writes, "Every time we look at a photograph, we are aware, however slightly, of the photographer selecting that sight from an infinity of other possible sights. This is true even in the most casual family snapshot." John Berger, *Ways of Seeing* (New York: Viking Press, 1973), 10.

5. Ken Wilber, *Eye to Eye*, preface.

6. For a discussion of the concept of "seeing-as" as used in philosophy and as applied to the study of religion and theology, see Garrett Green, *Imagining God* (San Francisco: Harper and Row, 1989).

7. A concept developed by the American philosopher William James (1842–1910).

8. For an integrated, interdisciplinary perspective on the various ways the world is schematized, see Michael A. Arbib and Mary B. Hesse, *The Construction of Reality* (Cambridge: Cambridge University Press, 1986).

9. Joseph Campbell, *The Hero with A Thousand Faces*, Bollingen Series no. 17, 2d ed. (Princeton, N.J.: Princeton University Press, 1968), 381.

10. The best overview description I have seen of "speech-act" theory for purposes of religious studies, is Terrence Tilley, "Part One: Speech-Act Theory," in *The Evils of Theodicy* (Washington, D.C.: Georgetown University Press, 1991). The idea that language can be understood as an act is arrived at by the two major streams of modern philosophy, those represented by Ludwig Wittgenstein and Martin Heidegger. For a lucid presentation of their respective contributions relative to the contextuality of interpretation, see Charles Guignon, "Philosophy After Wittgenstein and Heidegger," *Philosophy and Phenomenological Research* 1, no. 4 (June 1990), 649–672.

11. An important collection of essays on the varieties, vices, and virtues of relativism is Michael Krausz, ed., *Relativism: Interpretation and Confrontation* (Notre Dame, Ind.: University of Notre Dame Press, 1989). Also useful for a review of issues is Jack W. Meiland and Michael Krausz, eds., *Relativism: Cognitive and Moral* (Notre Dame, Ind.: University of Notre Dame Press, 1982). A theological overview is Joseph Runzo, *Reason, Relativism and God* (New York: St. Martin's Press, 1986). A sympathetic treatment of relativism as a human, cultural necessity is Paul Feyerabend, *Farewell to Reason* (London: Verso, 1987), 19–89.

12. David Tracy, citing Simone de Beauvoir's characterization of passive pluralism as "the perfect ideology for the modern bourgeois mind," in *Plurality and Ambiguity: Hermeneutics, Religion, Hope* (San Francisco: Harper and Row, 1987), 90.

13. The literary critic Wayne Booth uses the term to represent a way of learning from the plurality of interpretations of literature without reducing them to yet another outside theory. The pluralist approach to different exegeses of a poem would thus recognize the reasoning process of each on its own terms, the validity of two or more interpretations, and yet also the possibility of invalid interpretations ("the Garden of Eden story is about polar bear mating habits"). For his analysis of this and various other kinds of pluralistic approaches to literary meaning see his *Critical Understanding: The Powers and Limits of Pluralism* (Chicago: University of Chicago Press, 1979).

Index

"Age of Enlightenment," 16
Alchemy, 59
Alcoholics Anonymous, 63
Alienation, religion as expression
  of social, 18–20
Allah, 96
Animism theory, 17–18, 80
Apollo, 65
Archetype(s): self, 54–55, 64; of
  unconscious, 51–55
Aristotle, 114
Asceticism, 21; religiousness and,
  122
Asian religions, 27, 61, 67, 80,
  81, 82. See also Confucianism;
  Taoism
Atheists, 15
Athena, 93
Audience, as context, 116–18
Australian aboriginals, 33
Autonomy, 51, 52–53
Awareness, levels of, 105–6

Baha'i, 90
Baha'u'llah, 90
Bali, 77, 78
Bhagavad Gita, 71
Bible, 10, 25, 81, 90, 101, 117.
  See also Scripture
Biblical religions, 56–59, 81–82.
  See also Christianity; Islam;
  Judaism
Biology, 8
Black Muslim sect, 41
Bodhisattvas, 96–97
Brahman, 96
Brazil, 43
Buber, Martin, 106

Buddha(s), 31, 55, 59, 71, 90;
  Amida, 41; believing in, 75;
  enlightenment of, 77, 98;
  historical view of, 91; as the
  Lord, 77; teaching of, 40, 97,
  102, 105
Buddhism, 6, 8, 37, 56, 61, 92;
  and comparative religion, 78,
  79, 81, 82; criticism of
  Christianity by, 95; and
  enlightenment, 82, 88, 90,
  91, 103–5; historical
  formation of, 40–41, 90–91;
  Mahayana, 91, 103, 105; Pure
  Land, 41; Shingon, 98, 104,
  105; Theravada, 105; and
  universalism, 96–97; versions
  of, 43, 75; Zen, 101, 105

Calvin, John, 16
Catholic Church, 5, 94, 99
Catholicism, 13, 90, 99
Causes, meanings vs., 10–11
Centers of world, 77, 79, 89
Chemistry, 8
Christianity, 37, 38, 56, 68; and
  comparative religion, 78, 81–
  82; and definition of religion,
  5; historical formation of, 89–
  90; redemptive element of,
  40; varieties of interpretation
  of, 92–95; versions of, 43. See
  also Catholic Church;
  Catholicism; Protestantism
Christian Science, 90
Christmas, 35
Churingas, 31
Coles, Robert, 116

Comparative religion, 6, 13, 67–68; interplay of similarity and difference in, 75–80; reflections on frame of, 83–86; and religion as subject matter, 69–75; and typologies of different kinds of religion, 80–83

Compatibility, question of, 125–31

Confucianism, 37, 81, 82, 104, 115, 121

Confucius, 71

Context, 27

Contextuality of interpretation, 110–11; interpreter's audience, 116–18; multiple meanings, 114; places and views, 111–13; reflecting on, 123–24; situation of interpreter, 115–16; timing, 113–14; varieties and paradoxes of religiousness, 121–23; varying object of interpretation, 118–21

Conversion, 26, 63

"Daimon," 55

Dalai Lama, 94

Darwin, Charles, *The Origin of Species*, 17

Deism, 17, 95

Dependency, 51, 52

Differences, understanding, in comparative religion, 78–80

Dionysius, 65

Diversity, religious interpretations of religious, 91–97

Divination, practice of, 10

Divine vs. human origins of religion, 18–22, 27

"Documentary hypothesis," 23

Dogon tribe (Africa), 102–3

Dreams, 50, 62

Durkheim, Emile, 44, 45, 48, 50, 61–62; *The Elementary Forms of the Religious Life*, 29–32; and ritual, 34–35

East Asian religions, *see* Asian religions

Easter, 77, 88

Ecclesiastes, 113

Eckhart, Meister, 106–7

Ecstasy, religiousness and, 42, 121–22

Ego, 48, 49, 50–51; development, stages of, 51–55; and unconscious, religious piety and relationship of, 61–63

Eliade, Mircea, 74, 80, 84, 85, 114; on aim of historian of religion, 69, 83; on religion as subject matter, 69–70; on the sacred, 71

Enlightenment, 82, 88, 90, 91; Buddhist levels of, 103–5

Environment, as relational term, 7

Ethics, religiousness and, 122

Evidence, imagination and, 12

Evolutionism, 13, 17; spiritual, 105–6

Existence, religion and, 135

Existentialism, 106

Faith, religiousness and, 122

Feminist interpretation of religion, 25

Festivals, 35, 36

Feuerbach, Ludwig, *The Essence of Christianity*, 18–19

Frazer, James G., 18

Freud, Sigmund, 13, 48, 51, 54, 65; and unconscious, 20–22, 48–49; his view of religion, 20–22, 116

Fuji, Mount, 112

Fundamentalism, 39–40

Galileo, 25

Garden of Eden, 11, 52–53, 55, 99

Geertz, Clifford, 46

Ghost Dance movement, 41

Gnostic movement, 24, 58–59, 90

God(s), 55; "death of," 18; mythologies and, 33–34; as projection of humanity, 18–19; and slavery, 25

Goddesses, kings and, 55–56

Gospel(s), 24, 82, 89; of John, 24, 98

Griaule, Marcel, 102–3
Gunung Agung (Bali), 77, 78
Guru, 107

Heretics, philosophical, 15
Hermeneutical circle, 116
Hermitism, 42
Hick, John, 93–94
Hinduism, 61, 75, 96, 98, 103;
    and comparative religion, 81,
    82; historical formation of, 90
Historical materialism, 24
Historicism, 24
Hokusai, 112
Homer, 5
Human vs. divine origins of
    religion, 18–22, 27
Hume, David, 17

Imagination, evidence and, 12
India, religions originating in, 81,
    82. See also Buddhism;
    Hinduism
Innovation, institutionalization
    and, 38–39
Integration, 51, 53
Interpretation(s) of religion, 6,
    135; as act, 132–33; critical,
    15–16; as form of behavior,
    12–13; formation of religion
    through, 89–91; forms and
    purposes of, 9–13; religious,
    of religious diversity, 91–97.
    See also Contextuality of
    interpretation
Introspection, religiousness and,
    122
Islam, 40, 43, 68, 81–82, 90

James, William, 129; The Varieties
    of Religious Experience, 63, 75
Jaspers, Karl, 106
Jesus Christ, 31, 71, 77, 81, 90,
    96; and historical formation of
    Christianity, 89; sufferings of,
    97; as symbol of self, 59–61
Job, 56, 61
Jones, Jim, 120
Joyce, James, Ulysses, 112–13
Judaism, 37, 40, 68, 81–82, 89, 92

Judgment, suspension of, in
    comparative religion, 73–74
Jung, Carl Gustav, 48, 116; and
    archetypes of unconscious,
    51–55; interpreting history of
    religion by, 55–61, 63–66;
    and psyche as matrix, 49–51;
    and religious piety and
    relationship of ego and
    unconscious, 61–63; and
    unconscious, 48–49

Kaaba (Mecca), 77, 78
Kabbala, 100
Kierkegaard, Søren, 106
Kings, goddesses and, 55–56
Krishna, 71, 77

Language(s): lens of religious, 87–
    89; of religion, 70–71;
    transcending, 101–2; view of,
    as habitats, 7
Liminality, 35
Lotus Sutra, 77

Magic, 18
Mahakasyapa, 101
Marx, Karl, 13, 22, 28, 48; on
    religion, 19–20, 24
Marxism, 8, 13, 19, 20, 22
Mary, 61; Assumption of, 58
Masai, 35
May, Rollo, 106
Meaning(s), 11–12; causes vs.,
    10–11; levels of religious, 97–
    102
Meditation: societies, 36;
    techniques, 101–2
"Megachurch," 43
Ministries, television, 43
Monasticism, 52
Monotheism, 8, 26, 27, 61, 68, 80
Mormonism, 90
Moses, 23, 81, 90, 92, 99, 117;
    laws of, 98, 101
Muhammed, 31, 39, 77, 81, 90
Müller, F. Max, 67–68
Muslims, 36, 77, 96. See also Islam
Mythology(ies): and gods, 33–34;
    stages of, 51–55

Nagarjuna, 103–4
Negative functions of religion, 24–25
New Year festivals, 36, 77
Nietzsche, Friedrich, 18, 106
Night of Power, 77
Nihilism, 133
Nirvana, 56, 91, 93, 105
Noah's ark, 93

Oedipus complex, 21, 51
"Other, the," 80
"Overbeliefs," 129

Paganism, 68, 76, 80, 92–93
Paradigms, 4–5
Patterns, understanding, in comparative religion, 77–78
Paul, Saint, 60, 89
Peoples Temple, 119, 120, 121
Peter (first Pope), 99
Phenomenon, religion seen as, 73–74
Phenomenology of religion, 74–75
Philo of Alexandria, 117
Physics, 8
Plains Indians, 41, 107
Plato, 95
Platonism, 101, 103
Pluralism, 3, 4, 93–94, 125, 134
Points of view, about religion, 1–5
Polytheism, 80, 92
Positivism, 18
Possession cult, 42
Protestantism, 5, 13, 39, 90, 99
Proteus, 132
Psyche, 48, 86; as matrix, 49–51
Psychoanalysis, 48, 49, 65
Psychology, 13; and archetypes of unconscious, 51–55; and concept of unconscious, 48–49; and interpreting history of religion, 55–61; and psyche as matrix, 49–51; reflecting on frame of, 63–66; and religious piety and relationship of ego and unconscious, 61–63
Purity, 79; rules, 37

Qur'an, Holy, 31, 77, 81–82

Ramadan, 77
Rastafarians, 41–42
Rationalism (rationality), 16–18, 77, 106
Reciprocity: model, 131–33; principle, 106–7, 109
Redemption, religions of, 40, 41
Relationships, religion as projection of unconscious, 20–22
Relativity, facing new, 133–34
Religion(s): Asian, 27, 61, 67, 80, 81, 82; assessment of criticisms of, 25–27; biblical, 56–59, 81–82; definition of, 5–6, 85–86, 126; and existence, 135; human vs. divine origins of, 18–22, 27; interpreting, 6; negative functions of, 24–25; originating in India, 81, 82; as primitive thought, 16–18. *See also* Comparative religion; Psychology; Religious interpretation of religion; Society
Religious interpretation of religion, 13–14, 87; and formation of religion through interpretation, 89–91; and lens of religious language, 87–89; and levels of religious meaning, 97–102; and levels of religious understanding, 102–7; reflections on frame of, 107–9; and religious interpretations of religious diversity, 91–97
Religiousness, varieties and paradoxes, of, 121–23
Repression, intellectual, religion and, 25
Rig Veda, 96
Rites: of passage, 36; renewal, 35
Ritual: sacred, 71; as social expression, 34–37

Sabbath, 32, 33
Sacred(ness), 30–32, 41, 85; religion and, 71–73

Sacrifice, religiousness and, 122
Salvation-type religions, 40
Sannyasin(s), 42
Science: challenge to religious models from, 3; and Deism, 17; languages of religion and, 8, 30; for organization and perception, 5
Scripture: interpreting, 98–101; as product of human history, 22–24
Self: archetype, 54–55, 64; Christ as symbol of, 59–61
Servetus, Michael, 16
Shadow projection, 57–58
Shakespeare, William, 4, 8
Shamanism, 63
Shroud of Turin, 125
Sioux Indians, 98
Skepticism, 131
Social organization, religion and historical forms of, 37–38
Social syntheses, religious systems as, 42–43
Society, 13, 28, 86; applications of sociological frame, 33–37; kinds of, and kinds of religion, 37–43; reflections on social frame, 44–47; religion vs., 39–42; religious function of, 32; as source of religion, 29–32
Sociological frame: applications of, 33–37; reflections on, 44–47
Sophia, 58
Sri Ramakrishna, 96
Strict relativism, 131
Subjectivism, 131
Suicide, mass, at Jonestown, Guyana, 119–20
Supernatural, 18, 27, 28, 29, 63

Talmud, 99
Tao, 82, 96, 101
Taoism, 81, 82, 96, 101, 104

Tao Te Ching, 101
Ten Commandments, 71, 89
Thought, religion as primitive, 16–18
Tillich, Paul, 88, 106
Time magazine, 116
Torah, 31, 77, 82, 89, 102; interpreting, 99–100
Totemic principle, 30–31
Tylor, Edward B., 17
Typologies of different kinds of religion, 80–83

Umbanda, 43
Unconscious, 24; archetypes of, 51–55; Freud and, 20–22, 48–49; Jung and, 48–49, 50–51; religious piety and relationship of ego and, 61–63
Understanding: concept of, 11–12; levels of religious, 102–7
Unification Church, 90
Universalism, varieties of, 95–97
Upanishads, 61, 90, 98

Vedas, 90, 96, 115
Viewpoints, about religion, 1–5

Weber, Max, 37, 46
Wisdom, religiousness and, 122
World: centers of, 77, 79, 89; configuring of, 6–9; religion vs. society or, 39–42

Xenophanes, 20–21

Yahweh, 56–57
Yin and yang, 53, 61, 79
Yom Kippur, 32, 35

Zeus, 92–93
Zohar, 100
Zuni Mountains (New Mexico), 33, 77